All because the
lady loves…
Wedding Cake

PETRA KLUSKE

authorHOUSE®

AuthorHouse™
1663 Liberty Drive
Bloomington, IN 47403
www.authorhouse.com
Phone: 1-800-839-8640

First published by AuthorHouse   01/04/2012

ISBN: 978-1-4678-7966-8 (sc)
ISBN: 978-1-4678-7967-5 (ebk)

ACKNOWLEDGEMENTS

In January 2010, I set myself the challenge of writing a book, going along to a night school to pick up a few tips. I didn't start putting pen to paper until some nine months later. The book has taken me just over a year to complete and has been achievable with the help and enthusiasm from my friends and family. Donna, Liz, Jane, Jeannie, Natasha and Uncle John, thank you for all your efforts in taking the time and trouble to read my book and be my harshest critics, ensuring that I get the story just right! Matt, in parts, this is our story and I thank you for your support and encouragement throughout our time together. Ian, thank you for working with my ideas to create the book cover. Sophie, I had such fun shooting the final photograph. You knew it had to be perfect and you got it spot on.

The author is a middle-aged serving police officer. She does not have any literary accolades or university degrees to boast, but having spent so much of her service writing police statements, says she has in many ways been a ghost writer to victims and witnesses of crime. Having lived through some challenging life experiences, she decided the time had come to write a story of her own. Although this her first novel, is written in the style of an autobiography, the author is not claiming it is factual. She suggests it may be based on some real life events, but it is for the reader to decide for themselves what is fact or fiction, if some, all or any.

It's better to regret the things you do, than to regret the things you didn't do.

PROLOGUE

"Hi Michelle, it's Sadie . . . How ya' going?" said the chirpy girly voice at the end of the phone.

"Good thanks."
I said in an excited but slightly nervous tone.

Although I'd been expecting Sadie's call at any time, I still felt unprepared and unsure how I should feel about it.

"I have your first job. You are to meet Ralphy and collect one hundred and twenty, with a negative twenty. Any extra you get is all yours."

I pulled over to scribble down the details of where I was to go that following day. With a wish of Good Luck from Sadie, the call ended.

I checked on the street map to find the location an hour or two drive away South. I could not be more precise than that at the time, as I was unfamiliar with the route and not entirely confident about my transport. I left with plenty of time to get there, but managed to get disorientated and lost the way. Suddenly time became tight and I began to panic. I didn't want to mess this up. I had to get it right. I had to get there.

1

As I drove down the dusty road in the middle of nowhere, I became a little hesitant as to whether I was doing the right thing or not. It had started to get dark and the atmosphere felt eerie as grass hoppers clicked and tumble weed bounced across my path. There was just enough light for me to make out the house numbers, most partially concealed with foliage. A cluster of cars were parked up at the side of the road. Number twenty-five . . . Got it!

I pulled over to double check that I definitely had the right house number and decided to park a few doors down from the other cars. I didn't want to get parked in, just in case I had to leave in a hurry. There I was with a sensible head on, yet I was about to do something out of character and utterly crazy.

I adjusted the mirror to check I was looking okay. I checked my watch. I was still a little early and with enough time for a cigarette. I pulled out a new packet of twenty-five Marlborough Lights, loving the fact that they actually cost less than I'd usually pay for a packet of twenty. The flame quivered as I held it up to one of my free cigarettes. Drawing back a deep breath of tobacco, hearing the crackling of the burning stick, I held my breath for longer than usual, then exhaled slowly, savouring every second, delaying time. It was no good. I couldn't stall it off any longer. I picked up my holdall on the front seat and got out of the car. I tried to keep my thoughts empty as I clip-clopped up to the front door and took little notice of the face that opened it to me. Following Sadie's instructions, I collected my money up front. I was shown into a bedroom and instructed that when ready, I was to make my way out to the shed in the rear yard.

There was still time for me to pull out of this. It seemed madness that I'd put myself in this position, when only two weeks earlier I'd been pounding the streets in my uniform and comfortable shoes. Yes, I needed a job here, but there were other options. Okay, I'd have to work lots more hours, but it would be respectable, rather than this illicit method of earning a quick buck. I checked my watch . . . Seven minutes to go. I went back outside, lighting another free one. Pacing three steps to the left, three steps to the right . . . Checking the watch again, five more minutes. Another heavy drag and I was out of time. I went back to the bedroom. My throat dry and tight, breathing rapid, chest thumping and arms unsteady. This was it. No turning back. Skirt down, top off, shoulders back and perk up those boobs. It's show time!

CHAPTER ONE

CHANGING ROOMS

THE GARDEN LOOKS AMAZING in its morning dewing brightness, as the sun blazes through the multi-coloured leaded glass boarder of the kitchen window. It can take over an hour to mow the lawn and even longer to trim back the tall foliage boarders of this corner plot, but it's worth the effort. 36 Stone Lodge Mews is a detached house built in the 1970's and true to the rather bland architectural style of that time. With five bedrooms, open planned lounge-diner, double garage and two bathrooms, it's a mansion in comparison to the poky one bedroomed townhouse we'd come from in London and it feels quite an achievement to own such a lovely property at the tender age of twenty-six. My husband Neil and I bought the property at a knock down price, because it was in need of an upgrade. I enthusiastically embrace the challenge of this DIY project, watching the many TV home improvement shows whilst flicking through the piles of House Beautiful magazines stashed beside the bed. I day dream that perhaps our home will one day feature in one of those magazine before and after write ups, so keep a scrap book with photographs of some of my own DIY achievements and cuttings of my favourite ideas. I feel committed, determined and focused in my efforts. There's a feeling of great promise and hope for future happiness and contentment. The master plan is to one day have this as our family home, with all the hustle and bustle that goes with it. I fantasise that we'll have two children—a girl called Jessica Leigh and a boy called Frederick John. They're going to be good looking kids, after all, we're a good looking couple, both relatively tall—5'7" and 6'1". We're both of proportionate build and although my weight fluctuates by about a stone, I'm always around a size 12-14 and into my fitness, so feel our off-spring will follow suit. I plan what bedrooms they're going to have and how I'll decorate them. One of the garages could be converted into the playroom and we'll have the swings and slides in the garden, after all, it is the size of a small park. Perhaps we'll employ a nanny. Everything will be fabulous and we'll live happily ever after.

So, here I am gazing out of the kitchen window, but there's work to be done. I'm suitably dressed, radio on, cup of tea made, white spirit and paint brushes to hand, all set for another day on the home improvement project. My decorating clobber consists of my old tracky bottoms and one of Neil's tatty rugby tops. They're splattered with crusted globs of paint in various colours and densities. My blonde bobbed hair is currently untamed, with a slight wave to it, which has shaped itself into headphones and has tiny white dots attached from the previous days ceiling paint. The tops of my fingernails have gloss paint firmly embedded and no matter how many times I scrub my hands with white spirit, it's not going to budge; it just makes my hands more dry and cracked. I have to peel my right hand open to hold my tea cup, as it's still wedged firmly in a fist from the hours of paint scraping the previous day. The edges of my lips are chapped and scabby. I run my tongue around them, in an effort to add some moisture, but this doesn't really help them to heal. It's my own fault though. I should really have worn a face mask when I was sanding the stairs. It's true to say that I'm not looking at my best, but I don't care that much. I have a job to do and that's my priority for now.

So, with the paint brush in hand, I begin the next stage of the transformation of the kitchen units. I prime them in silver paint, followed by a layer of Crackle Glaze. The next step is to brush lightly over with the lime green emulsion and hopefully this paint effect will work just like Laurence Llewelyn-Bowen suggests. Neil leaves the decorating to me and I don't mind too much, after all, it had been my choice to move to the county and he regularly reminds me of this.

"Look what I've given up so you can live near your family."
"I'm having to wear a blue shirt and work with these country bumpkins."
"All my friends are in London."
"I've had to take a pay cut to do this for you."

He's taken up new hobbies such as shooting and diving, which sometimes take him away for the weekend. I encourage this, as I want this move to be a success for us both and for him to come to the resolve that it has been a good relocation to make. I'm keen to press on with the transformation of our home so as to surprise and impress him on his return. I'm too busy to ever feel lonely and the radio serves as company and entertainment during the long tedious hours I'm spending painting, glossing, scraping and varnishing. The local radio station plays a good mix of songs from the previous decades and I reminisce on my past and congratulate myself on how far I've come.

"Save all your kisses for me, save all your kisses for me, bye bye baby, bye bye . . ."

Now that's an old one! I sing along to it as I know all the words. I picture being with my dad. It was just us and I felt really special and grown up being in the front seat of his car. He would point out the factory where he worked, as we drove to the shop to get his cigarettes. He would give me ten pence to buy some penny sweets, which was enough to buy twenty Black Jacks or Fruit Salads if I wanted to. I might even get some Space Dust. We'd pick something like a Marathon or Space Bar for my brother Steve, as they were the same price.

Steve was eighteen months younger than me and I guess just like any other brother and sister of a young age, we'd have some really good fights, mastering techniques such as thumb pressing of the eye ball, finger hook in the side of the mouth, Chinese burns and even an unimaginative hair pulling session. One of my specialities was to pin his arms and legs down, then lick the end of his nose and blow, causing the effect of an intolerable itch. In spite of this we also played well together. We would have Kick Start style cycling competitions when we'd set up an obstacle course in the garden. I'd make red and blue rosettes and certificates for us both and somehow, I'd manage to be a competitor and judge, which would explain why my pin board contained all the red rosettes.

Steve made a much needed companion when it came to the many house moves we made. By the time I'd reached sixteen we'd moved house and area eight times. With every move we were encouraged to dispose of our possessions and start afresh. We had to get used to the daunting challenge of new schools and making new friends. Yes, all this was good character building, but I do not think it helped to install stability, nor encourage or enable long term relationships. One move was made when I was only just sixteen and about to take my O-levels. A new school can be quite a hostile place at that age and few are willing to befriend the new girl unless you are a bit of a rebel or the classroom clown. I was neither. I'd spend lunch hours in the library doing homework as I'd have few friends to hang out with. Having completed homework in school time, I'd be free to do after school jobs.

I've always been a worker. As soon as I hit thirteen, I started my morning paper round. It would take me just over an hour every day, paying me a wage of five pounds per week. Four weeks wage enabled me to buy my prize possession—a Casio calculator wrist watch. Mum was a Care Assistant on and off during my childhood and she suggested I too go for a job in residential care. By the age of fourteen, I was working in an old people's home for a couple of hours after school each day and one full day during the weekend. My role would include getting residents up, washed and dressed, helping them on and off the commode, with any necessary wiping assistance given, cleaning the rooms and serving the meals.

Working in the local supermarket and taking on a second paper round all added to my teenage employment record, along with working on a market stall and in a haberdashery. The money rolled in and I became a loyal customer of Burlington and Great Universal catalogues, with my instalments paid on time during the given twenty week period. I was the first person in my school year to have a leather jacket. Even back then it cost me two hundred pounds, which seems madness as they are so much cheaper these days. I'd proudly wear this jacket, complete with trendy fitted shoulder pads, in the queue to collect my pink free meal ticket.

During my teenage years, Dad spent quite some time unemployed, but he'd be involved in work for the church. In between her work in care homes, mum would work as a VDU (visual display unit) operator in banks and building societies, apparently to get good rate employee mortgages. Dad had previously worked in factories. I remember my primary school teacher struggling to hold back her laughter when I announced that Dad made toilet seats for a living and proudly showed her the miniature toilet seat key ring fobs I possessed in various colours. During periods of unemployment, Dad would go on training courses to learn skills such as welding and carpentry. He had a well paid job as a cladding fitter for a short period, but got a huge shock when he found himself unable to pay the tax bill. Even though he'd never had great jobs, we always lived in nice houses because Mum and Dad would buy a house that needed renovating, do the necessary work, then sell it on at a profit. That's probably where my interest and skills in the world of house decorating evolved.

With the kitchen units finished in the vintage crackled effect, it's on to the floor boards, which I mask off with a criss-cross pattern and wood stain the individual panels in Jacobean Walnut and Antique Pine, using a sponge to smear across the boards . . .

We're heading for something, somewhere I've never been, sometimes I am frightened, but I'm ready to learn 'bout the Power of Love, Oh the Power of Love."

That's the Jennifer Rush ballad mum would always cry to; not for a love of my dad or some distant romance or affair, but for Peter, the Jack Russell Terrier that they had put to sleep whilst he was still fit and healthy. Peter had been with our family for as long as I could remember. He was not the most loyal of pets and would take any opportunity to escape from a gap in the fence or an open door. Many a time we'd go chasing after him and only have a chance of catching him when he'd stop to pick a fight with another much bigger dog. With the arrival of a new sibling and one accidental scratch too many, he had to go and for a time we all struggled with that loss, especially mum.

Mum did not appear to be comfortable showing us physical affection, nor would she declare her love for us as Dad did. However, she would share her attention with us in other ways. She'd take us on long country walks, picking corn or blackberries, perhaps we'd return home to make corn dollies and pies, whilst munching on her sugar sandwiches.

With the town carnivals came fancy dress competitions and we'd be sure to win with Mum's creativity in designing us the most original costumes. I recall that she perched a light blue shower cap on my head, with a small sock inside and hair band on top to create a bun, eyeliner pencilled across my forehead and sides of eyes, stockings wrinkled around my ankles, walking stick in hand and there I was, transformed into Ethel, the not so glamorous granny aged nine.

Mum was a completely different character to Dad. She was the creative and wacky one, who drew pictures of fairies with pixy faces and long hair that curled at the ends. She'd tell us that they lived in toad stools at the bottom of the garden and at times I'd be convinced that she really believed this. She'd look at the palms of our hands or perhaps into her crystal ball and tell us that we were going to achieve great things.

I never quite understood why Mum would rush into school clutching a tea towel, having been called in to collect me when I was having yet another nose bleed. Mum would tell me the reason for this reoccurring event was because my nose was growing. She would have her herbal remedy books to hand and come up with her own diagnosis to most medical conditions. She'd willingly write a letter to the teachers to excuse us from lessons and would brush off the fact that we had mastered forging her signature, so we could write our own notes if need be. Mum would declare that I was the musical one in the family and persuasively suggest that I entertain guests with a little something like Chopsticks on the piano, followed by Portsmouth on the recorder then Streets of London on the guitar, so that we could all sing along at the end of this mini-concert.

"The sound of your heart bleeding . . ."

There were other times when Mum would cry and say she was depressed. I would have been no more than ten years old when she got me to phone her place of work saying,

"Mummy can't make it into work today because she isn't well."

Sometimes Mum would scream as Dad was smashing up some household item, such as a plate or a food blender. We'd be sent to our rooms with the words from Dad,

"That's it . . . I'll get Peter put down!"
and I'd sob
"Please don't, pleeeeeeease, don't have Peter put down."

I'd huddle myself into a foetal position under the covers to muffle the sounds of yet another plate crashing against the wall, Christmas tree getting torn down or my guitar being battered to the ground. Of course it would all eventually end with excuses from Dad saying,

"The kids . . ." or *"Your mother . . ."*
was to blame for this apparent justified outburst. Dad would then be gushing with declarations of love for us all and we'd

go out to buy bigger, better items to replace those that had been destroyed.

With the bedroom floor now creatively stained and varnished, the walls brushed with the distressed effect, next comes the stencilling. Time goes so quickly when I'm having this much fun. The radio keeps playing those great tunes . . .

"We're in the army now . . . Ohhhhh, oooo, we're in the army . . . now."

My dad always had an interest, or perhaps I should rephrase that, he had an obsession with all things military. He'd tell us that he'd wanted to join the army after leaving school, but his mother had prevented him from doing so; she didn't want to see him killed as his father had been in the war. We'd repeatedly hear all about our heroic grandfather's D-Day death, but little about his actual life. We'd visit war graves, watch the war films and hear the war stories. In his late-thirties, dad joined the Territorial Army. He would train us up with his new found skills and we'd form part of his regiment, being taught to march and stand to attention, whilst being referred to as Private. He tied a thick length of rope between two trees in our garden and instructed us on the art of Regain. We'd start by hanging under the rope by our hands and ankles. We'd need to hoik a leg up and over the rope, to pull ourselves on top, then start the traverse along the length, keeping one leg dangling down, with the other bent and ankle pushing against the rope to aid balance.

Camping trips would become military survival missions. We'd have the basic provisions and comforts, plan hikes with a map and a compass, then stop on the way to cook beans on a Hexamine burner. We'd make up our survival kits, made from one of Dad's Golden Virginia tobacco tins filled with a pink water purifying tablet, waxed matches, a tin opener that resembled a razor blade in size and shape, a length of green string, needle and cotton and an AB biscuit. This snack was packaged in green foil and resembled a dog treat in flavour and texture.

During our childhood, outdoor pursuits prevailed. Along with the camping came canoeing, boating and cycling. With Dad's welding skills, he made us the most fabulous Go-Kart and we were the envy of the kids in the neighbourhood, who all then wanted to be our friends. Dad would give us some boxing tips and suggest that if someone got on the wrong side of us, we should offer up a fist to their face, look them straight in the eye and ask,

"Want some of that?"

Mum on the other hand would disapprove of such violent methods and scorn Dad for suggesting such things.

I am conscious that I am making my dad sound like some kind of ogre, which he was not. As a child, yes, he could be very intimidating; however with him it's a case of all things to an extreme and he could also be very affectionate and caring. He'd claim he was not the academic type and indeed remind us that we should be proud of our working class roots, discouraging us from ever considering university as an option. Yet I remember him sitting with me for hours, teaching me general arithmetic, the phonetic alphabet and the art of map reading. On a Sunday he'd be my much needed helper to deliver those heavy Sunday supplements during my cold morning rounds. Over the years, he dedicated so much effort assisting with my home improvements and saving me a fortune on skilled tradesmen. However, during times when I have fallen out of his favour, he has proved to be a cantankerous stubborn bully.

A cheap upgrade of the bathroom involves priming and painting the tiles. The tile paint needs to go on with speed otherwise it goes streaky. I've turned up the radio so I can still hear it from upstairs . . .

"He looked at me, and then I blushed, coz I remember when I loved him so much, Frankie . . . do you remember me? Frank-kie-eee."

I was singing and dancing to that one in the early 80's at the church play, when I was dressed in a badly made jazz blue coloured nylon dress with an egg yolk yellow tie around it, playing the part of a telecom girl.

We moved to Sussex when I was eleven and with a new house and area came a new lifestyle. A pair of young American Mormon Missionaries had charmed their way into our family and I soon became Sister Michelle and did baptisms for the dead at the East Grinstead Temple. Tea, coffee and cola were considered drugs due to their caffeine content, so we took to drinking Shloer and a hot drink called Barley Cup, which was a bad tasting coffee substitute. Alcohol was forbidden, which was no great loss as my parents were never really drinkers. A great achievement for my dad was to stop smoking, which was a relief to us all as we no longer had to tolerate him puffing away in the car with the windows closed. Monday was dedicated to Family Home Evenings. This involved us all being together and being given the opportunity to talk individually for ten to fifteen minutes about anything we wanted to. As head of the family, Dad would read us something from the Mormon Family Home Evening manual. This manual would offer some guidance about good Christian living and refer to the scriptures. We'd end with a prayer to Our Heavenly Father and be nice to one another for the rest of the evening.

Sex, drugs and rock'n'roll were off the agenda with chastity being held in high regard. No sex before marriage for those handsome young Mormon Missionaries, who were the role models to us teenagers in the church. Most were aged between nineteen to twenty-one, away from their homelands, dedicating two years of their lives to spread the words of the late Prophet, Joseph Smith. They'd be involved in the various clubs, discos or camping trips. Theatre productions proved great fun and enabled everyone to get involved, whether it be as a performer, singer, song or script writer, scene producer, musician or perhaps a ticket seller. These were big events in the church as they involved competing against the other branches of the church and we were all determined to win one of the many awards.

I look back with fond memories of my time in the church. It's my view that the Mormon church played a positive influence during my early teenage years. I would recommend the ways and lifestyle to any family. However, the club fees may not be so enticing, with a ten percent tithe expected from us all . . . And that includes pocket money!

With a new faith came new siblings and in my early teens Abby arrived, followed by Natasha eighteen months later. With young children in the household came additional responsibility. I took the opportunity to use my little sisters in my school project work in Parent Craft, studying their development and milestone achievements.

Discontentment with the faith started setting in for my dad. He'd tell us that he'd become aware that some of the parishioners were not all that they appeared to be. His faith in the Mormon church subsided and his taste for tobacco crept back. If it was good enough for him, then it was good enough for me. By the time I was fifteen, I was having those crafty Embassy cigarettes from a packet of ten, which I bought from the creepy looking man in the card shop, who appeared more than willing to serve children.

With the decline in faith came another house move and just before my sixteenth birthday we moved to a new area and another new school. As I mentioned before, this was a difficult time for me as I was in the process of taking O-levels and CSE's. To make matters worse, the new area did not run the same curriculum in all my chosen subjects, so I spent my final school months going between two schools.

Mum pointed out an advert in the local paper 'Au-pairs wanted in Switzerland.'

"How marvellous," she said,

"You'd make a fantastic Au-pair with all the experience you've had with Abby and Tasha. You could be like Heidi and live in the mountains and it would all be wonderful," she said.

"I always got by on my own . . . How can I leave you alone . . .
A . . . lone . . ."

That song by Heart is what I call The Ironing Song

Just a few weeks after I finished taking my exams, Dad and Steve saw me off at the airport with tearful goodbyes. I arrived in Zurich, Switzerland, instantly disappointed that there was not a mountain in sight. I was to live in a remote village where the local bus passed through just a couple of times a day, travelling to the nearest town some half an hour away. The family had a three year old daughter and I anticipated my duties would be centred around the care of this child. How wrong I was!

Within hours of my arrival at the family home, I was cutting the grass whilst the lady of the home sat doing lunch with one of her friends. My duties were to walk Filo, the large black crossbreed dog and to do the housework. I was given strict instructions as to how the housework was to be performed; a damp sponge cloth to dust all surfaces, vacuuming daily in all rooms, polishing the marble stairs and landing, along with clipping and watering the outdoor pot plants. The lady of the house was very specific as to how she wanted the ironing done, so that all items could be placed neatly into drawers and cupboards. Tea-towels were to be folded in three length ways, then folded once width ways. Socks had to be ironed flat, then placed on top of one another and folded once so that they were compact. Shirts and T-shirts were to appear as if they'd come straight from a shop . . . and so the list continued. Even underwear got ironed! These duties were performed whilst I was abandoned by the rest of the household, left on my own all day, rarely setting eyes on the three year old child.

At that time, all men of age in Switzerland were to do National Service and during my employment, I was even polishing the army boots and pressing the uniform. Meals were bland and predictable, with fruit flans on a Friday and bread and cheese being supper most days.

I'd only managed to achieve a grade 4 CSE in German and I suspect this only-just-passed grade was down to pot luck during those multi-guess exam questions. I had hoped I would at least learn the language as a resident in the country, after all I now had a Swiss bank account. However, the lady of the house announced that she was keen to improve her English language skills and never spoke German with me. When I did hear any of the language, it was spoken in Swiss German, complete with the strong dialect. I soon realised the only thing I was going to be learning was how to give a home a good clean and nothing more.

It was a lonely existence, but returning home to the UK was not an option as I would have felt such a failure.

The family I was with and probably the other 197 residents of the village were into horse riding. The closest I'd ever previously come to such an activity was a pony ride at a country fete. However, I was keen to be accepted and volunteered myself for a horse riding lesson, which was not my greatest success. Yasmin was huge in comparison to the horses ridden by the young school girls in my class. She must have sensed my fear, rearing up as I tried wrapping my arms around her neck. I slid off her body and that's when she took off. Everyone was chasing after her like something from a Benny Hill sketch. I half heartedly followed, although I had no intention of catching up with her as I knew then that Yasmin and I were not going to get along.

The Master of the stables was Herr Ralph, who was clearly well respected by the horsey villagers. He was a short weazly looking old man, with a tanned, wrinkled, weathered face and a jaw line that sank in as if he didn't have many teeth left. I had no idea what he was saying, but couldn't help noticing his spindly, twitchy little fingers. With his elbows bent and hands in front of him, level with his chest, he was all touchy-feely with those little girls. I was glad it had been a unsuccessful lesson, because I didn't like that grubby little man.

Routine set in and for one afternoon a week I went to language school for a couple of hours; not because the family wanted me to learn the language, but because that was set as part of the terms and conditions of employment. I began to have some sort of social life, even if it was for that short time once a week. As I met new people, we'd go to The Pickwick Pub after classes and share stories on how our jobs were going. It was then that I realised that I'd been served a rather raw deal and felt like the slave in comparison.

As the weeks progressed, I developed a good friendship with Katie, who was an American Au-pair a couple of years older than me. She was a plump looking girl with a warm heart and fun-loving nature. She would wear her trendy Guess jeans, the cosiest looking sheepskin coat and regularly check her bank account to see if her weekly allowance had come through from Daddy. On our days off we'd wander around the shops and snack on Bratwurst. Sometimes we'd get a train to some other town to check out another one of the Pickwick Pub chains. On an Au-pairs wage and at Swiss prices, there was no way we'd ever manage to drink to an extreme, but we did get a taste for the beer and found it was most economically purchased by the jug.

During my many days alone in the house, I'd look forward to the phone calls from Katie. She'd tell me that her family were cool about her using their phone. One day, she explained that she'd been discussing my plight with Gabi, her employer. Gabi had apparently told Katie that my employment deal did not sound as it should be. Katie told me that there was another family known to a friend of a friend of Gabi and they were looking for an Au-pair.

I'd now been with my own family for over four months, but one Sunday on my day off, on Katie's instruction, I travelled to Bern train station. At a set time and platform I was to meet the potential new family. I travelled the two hours to get there, only to find no one was there to meet me. I suddenly felt very vulnerable, disappointed and let down. I found a phone box on the platform and called Katie immediately. She answered calmly and confidently, explaining that it had all been arranged and I would be met. She began giving a description of who I was to look out for.

"Okay, there will be an old lady with her hair in a bun and she'll be with a little girl who is about five years old with blonde hair . . ."

On cue, those very images came walking towards my phone box, hand in hand. The old lady had a kindly face and I quickly regained confidence in the plan of action.

Frau Braun was her name and the little girl with the bobbed hair and cheeky wide smile was ironically named Heidi. We got on another train and about half an hour later we were at the door of a grand looking house opposite a church. I was introduced to Herr and Frau Meier, who were vicars and had three children aged one, three and five. After brief negotiations, it was agreed that I'd start work for them two weeks later.

That same evening, I returned back to Filo and the rest of the family. I wasn't sure what the correct procedure was when it came to wanting to leave this family; after all, I was still sixteen and inexperienced in such matters. I went to my room and began writing my letter of resignation, giving them two weeks notice. My hands were shaking as I put pen to paper and once the letter was done, I went up the cold marble staircase into the lounge, where I was never ever invited to sit. Both the lady of the house and her husband, who'd never speak to me, were sitting there. She asked how my day off had been as I nervously handed her the note.

"*Sie geht.*" she told her husband.

"*Was?*" he said in his deep gruff voice, which didn't really match his appearance.

The two went into an exchange of angry sounding words with one another, complete with lots of rolling of R's and throaty C's. She then turned to me and calmly yet spitefully uttered,

"*We do not need two weeks notice. You can go now.*"

I had not expected such a hostile response and I had no idea what I was supposed to do now. It was late in the evening and I had nowhere I could actually go. I hurried out of the house to the temporary sanctuary of a phone box where I called the Meier's. This family, who were some two hours away and barely knew me, instructed me to return to the home to pack my bags. Phone calls then followed between the soon to be old family and The Meier's. The following day I was dumped off at the nearest train station, never to return to that remote village again. On the way to Beil, I stopped at Zurich Airport train station to call my parents and update them, as they had no idea what had been going on. I'd given them no indication of problems before that time as I'd not wanted to worry them.

The Meier family were now away on holiday for a couple of weeks, but they'd arranged for me to stay with Herr and Frau Braun for now, who took on the role of my stand-in grandparents. I think they saw me as some poor abandoned charity case and they were scooping me up to save me. Perhaps they were. Herr Braun was a retired teacher and I was never too sure what Frau Braun had done in her younger years, but she was a Blue Peter fan's greatest dream. She had a craft room equipped with a sewing machine, felt and lots of sticky back plastic. She was the guru of Arts and Crafts. In the kitchen she'd be drying apples, making Lebkuchen biscuits using antique presses and baking yet another plaited Zopf loaf.

Herr and Frau Braun looked like one of those friendly old couples that you'd expect to see dressed in traditional costume, standing beside a timber house and milk urn on the advertising poster for a tin of Swiss chocolates. I have fond memories of this kindly couple, who I don't doubt have long since passed on.

So, just after my seventeenth birthday, I arrived at The Meier household and life in Switzerland was oh so different. Brigitte and Reinhold were a really cool couple . . . for vicars! The household buzzed and I felt an equal part of it; like the big sister to the three children. I was given a room at the top of the house with the most amazing view of the snowy mountains of the Grindelwald. My days would be spent with the children, sitting at a large round table with sheets of coloured paper, plastic scissors, pots of glitter and glue. We'd go for long walks and pick up twigs and leaves, then return to stick them to our monthly picture board. I'd make cakes in bulk and freeze them, so that Brigitte could grab them out of the freezer and claim to her Parishioners that she'd been busy baking them herself.

Brigitte was in her mid thirties and struggled with her weight. To make matters worse, she had a younger sister who was clearly the slim pretty one and Brigitte would occasionally get reminded of this by her equally slim attractive mother. She announced that she'd discovered a new fail safe diet which consisted of wheatmeal and steak. So, for a week or so, Brigitte took on this strange diet concept, which of course was doomed by the temptation of those cakes stacked high in the freezer.

For the first time in my life I became weight and calorie aware. During my time in Switzerland I'd become rather chubby, probably from all that bread, cheese and chocolate. In reality I was no more than a stone heavier than I should have been, but for a teenager, that was a tragedy. I too gave the wheatmeal diet a go, filled myself up with an endless supply of apples and took to jogging. The weight fell off and a couple of months later I was running the ten mile Bern Grand Prez.

I spent ages planning an inter-railing trip. This was a month long adventure travelling around Europe on trains and my reward to myself for my year long service in Switzerland. Unfortunately, Katie dropped out of this joint venture at the last minute, but that wasn't going to stop me from a great opportunity. Weeks in advance, I packed my little rucksack, complete with a tobacco tin survival kit. I had the route mapped out to cover Venice, Florence, Rome, Corfu, mainland Greece, Yugoslavia, Munich, Paris, Normandy and Amsterdam. Being without a companion encouraged me to make the effort to befriend fellow travellers, but at the same time be very aware of my personal safety. The trip was a success and ended back in Switzerland, where I was able to say farewell to The Meier's.

On my return to England, I started working for a bank. At that time jobs were plentiful and a young person would often have the choice to consider what employment they wanted. Banks were considered a safe and sound option. However, I quickly established that the words office work, boredom and mundane all appeared affiliated with The Bank, so I was glad to leave after seven months.

I'd worked hard during my teenage years to have a good mix of work experience to add to my CV. It hadn't been an easy achievement by any means, but after an entrance exam, assessment weekend, interviews and passing my physical test the second time around, I was finally accepted for my dream career!

The varnish and paint are now dry; it's time to pull off the masking tape and stack away those sticky pots with bent lids. The house is complete and looks beautiful. I guess it's time to switch off the radio, but not until the end of this song . . . I love this one. It reminds me of when I met Neil . . .

"Deep down, I'm still confused about you . . . I feel so in love, oh baby, what can I do, I've been thinking about you . . . Oo Oo Ooooooo"

CHAPTER TWO

LONDON BEAT

THE END OF MY journey on the Northern Line was marked with three tower blocks, a huge sports field, skid pan and daunting assault course . . . All in that order. A few minutes walk away was Hendon Police College and the first entrance was the Cadet Centre, which was to be my home for the following year. I felt privileged that I had been accepted into this elite establishment; after all I was one of only two hundred and fifty young people in the UK to be accepted every year.

The course was physically challenging, with P.T forming part of the daily routine. I excelled in the social development skills, with community service attachments to a drop-in centre for the homeless in Central London and working at a youth club on a notorious housing estate.

Cadet life was disciplined, having to be in the breakfast hall for 7am, ready for Flag Parade in full uniform by 8am for inspection, followed by a packed timetable of courses in social awareness, community relations, media and religious studies, with various P.T and swimming lessons in-between the classroom work. Us girls would be covered in bruises and grazes up the inner thighs from rope climbing and the weekly assault course. We'd be taken off to North Wales every couple of months for a week long trek across the remote wilderness. We'd have heavy rucksacks, beret, breaches, long socks and light blue itchy woollen shirts to rock climb, abseil and canoe in. The finale at the end of the fifty two week course was a grand passing out parade, headed by Drill Sergeant Pether, where we impressed our loved ones with our formation marching to The Thunderbirds Song and award ceremony, from which I picked up most of the medals as best achiever.

Following on from Cadets and still a teenager (only just), I moved on to be a Trainee Constable at the main police college. One of those on-site tower blocks became my home for a further twenty weeks. I was issued with my proper police uniform, complete with wooden truncheon, handbag, whistle and cape. In those days we even got a stocking allowance, but I'd break the unwritten rule and wear tights. Although I'd spent so much time surrounded by young lads at the Cadet Centre, I was now in the minority group as one of very few females, surrounded by lots of hot blooded men!

It was at training school that I met Neil. It was love at first sight for me as he stood out among the rest as my Mr Motorbike Man; at least I assumed he had a motorbike as he was holding a crash helmet. I pointed out this subject of desire to one of my ex-cadet friends, who enthusiastically told me that she knew him, having spent an introductory day with his class whilst we were still in cadets. She instantly became Miss Match-Maker and without hesitation set about introductions. That's how I got to meet Neil—The first true love of my life.

Neil seemed really into me. Within weeks he invited me to be his partner at his passing out parade and suggested we might even want to consider moving in together once we both left training school. He took me for weekends away and was keen to introduce me to his friends. Looking back, I see that a big attraction to Neil was that he was much older than the males I'd been around for the past year. He was four years my senior and seemed so much wiser in all things. I had just bought a new car, yet lacked the confidence to drive it around unfamiliar areas. Neil changed all that and within no time had me driving around Piccadilly Circus and Trafalgar Square like it was second nature. We'd go for trips away and have fun together, canoeing on The Thames or roller-blading in Hyde Park. Neil made me feel so wanted and I absolutely adored him.

For a while after leaving training school, we lived in our individual police section houses, consisting of a box room with enough space for a single bed, wardrobe, desk and one of those big heavy fire doors that would angrily slam shut. I spend most of my free time at his accommodation. Within six months of leaving training school, we were keen to have our own place together, but found the cost of renting comparable with a monthly mortgage, so opted on buying a small home together. Once committed financially, marriage seemed a natural progression and a few weeks before my twenty-second birthday I became Mrs Charles.

Being a married couple seemed to make little difference to our commitment to one another and life remained fun. We'd go to the various London clubs with friends, reaping the benefits of living just a few miles from the centre of town, which was a short taxi ride away. We'd have house parties and be entertained by friends. Money was a little tight, but nothing out of the ordinary for any couple in their early twenties with a mortgage, car loans and a pay scale relative to age and service. Financially, the major down side was that we were living in recession and the value of our house had fallen by twenty-five percent since we'd purchased it, so we were having to save up just to be able to move home again.

My career as a police woman was going well. I'd been posted to a station in South East London, with an easy commute into work. Taking my age and shifts into account, it was not unusual for me to party until 2am, go to sleep for a few hours, ready for a 6am start . . . apparently stone cold sober! This was completely achievable and I was more than able to carry on business as usual. I'd be on duty in my shiny black shoes and handbag, walking my beat. I'd hide behind my usual oak tree, situated on the junction of a bus lane and no right turn; waiting in preparation for those non law abiding citizens who would fall prey to that hideous crime against the highway code and do that cheeky no right turn, bus lane, or perhaps both. They'd find me stepping out in the road to give them a fixed penalty ticket. I'd proudly return to my

Sergeant with an impressive wad of completed tickets in an attempt to fulfil my targets and prove my worth.

After about a year's service I was allowed to drive one of those not so high performance cars, complete with a blue light. I became the proud police panda car driver of a Rover Metro. I'd spend my morning shifts driving to various homes to take reports of crimes such as, theft of car radio. This mundane task was broken up by me stopping the occasional dodgy looking motorist, achieved by me flashing the head lights and flicking on the blue light. With my exceptional communication and people skills, I'd be thanked for my time and trouble by those I'd given the traffic infringement tickets to and we'd go our separate ways. I'd continue on my journey, thanking yet another patient motorist for stopping abruptly on the roundabout to let me pass and another who'd perhaps pulled over on the road side to let me go on in front of them. It was a short time later that I'd realise the probable reason for this kindness was that I'd forgotten to switch off my blue light . . . Whoops!

I was a fresh faced, attractive, uniformed constable and would frequently be told that I looked far too young to be doing such a job. However, in later years, I find myself saying much the same to many of my junior colleagues. It would not be unusual for my sympathetic approach to a male victim of crime to be misinterpreted, resulting in them suggesting a date and asking for my phone number, which I'd remind them was 999. I became resilient to attending calls for assistance, where the callers answered the door inappropriately dressed in perhaps the baggiest, once white underpants, hand tucked down them, scratching their genitals, starting their conversation as if I knew all about their issues, because, they'd remind me, it was somewhere in my police records.

Much of my first years service was on the station front desk, checking driving documents or appeasing yet another one of the local nut cases in my sympathetic attentive manner. As Probationers, we'd be disappointed to get posted to the front desk for a shift, hoping instead to be racing around in the area car. However, front office work actually offered great experience and grounding for any new officer.

There were times when I'd be seconded from my own station to patrol areas around Embankment, Westminster and Whitehall, posted to a duty called Central London Aid. I'd spend an entire shift walking an area no bigger than my local supermarket; by the end of my tour I'd know exactly how many steps there were to each road and have been snapped by numerous Japanese tourists.

Another of my Central London shifts was on New Years Eve in Trafalgar Square. It was probably the most anti-social shift to be given, as we'd start on a non Bank Holiday, so would earn no extra money for the whole of the shift. I guess that's why officers young in service were used. I was posted to the searching area and as the thousands of party revellers crammed into the Square, unaware of the no alcohol rule, I'd carry out the most dreadful task, of confiscating their bottles of Bolle and toss them into the skip. This was understandably met with great anger and hostility on every occasion. Once the clock struck midnight and the fireworks were over, the crowds would be sent on their way. That's when the party began for the vagrants and homeless, clambering into the skips to retrieve the contraband.

Being a police officer inevitably means that we are faced with various dangers, whether that be from weapon bearing customers or from the environment and locations we find ourselves in. I've had a few near scrapes in my time and shudder from the memory that I once very nearly had my head guillotined. It was a night shift and I'd been given the most desirable of positions, as Operator in the Area Car. A call came out over the radio,

"Alarm activation at Cross Roads Cinema, believed suspects on premises."

We blue lighted it to the call, screeching to a halt, as first on scene to the grating shrill of the alarm and view of smashed glass frontage. My colleague had already leapt out before I'd even had the chance to unfasten my seat belt. He heroically sped off, through a four foot gap in the cinema door, with just a couple of vending machines to light up the spacious entrance hall. I followed on behind towards the smashed entrance door, taking just a moment to stop in my tracks as another police car arrived. Head lights illuminated the front of the cinema and it was only then that I glanced up to see a diagonal jagged blade of glass dangling from the top of the door frame where I was about to go through. Moments later it came crashing down.

We are trained to be safety aware and given tools for our protection. At that time, these tools consisted of a whistle, set of handcuffs and a wooden truncheon. The men were issued with a long hard wooden stick, whilst the WPC's were given the shorter shiny light wood variety, which was neatly concealed in a specially designed skirt pocket. The only realistic use for this ten inch object was to smash the occasional window; even then, it was not always that effective in this task.

Over the years the tools of the trade have improved and officers are now equipped with body armour, ridged handcuffs, extendable metal asp and CS spray. We are trained in the use of all these things, but just sometimes it can go wrong.

One summer month, whilst sweating profusely in my body armour and the cuffs doing their usual thing of digging into the right side of my hip, we went to the scene of a scuffle outside a pub. Attempts to reason with the inebriated thugs proved pointless, so we took to pulling them away from one another as a crowd of spectators gathered. Suddenly something wet hit my face, preventing me from being able to open my eyes. That was it, I assumed I must have had acid thrown in my face by one of the crowd and I'd been rendered blind, never to be able to see again. I hunched vulnerably at the side of a parked car, confused and sightless.

"Oops, sorry about that pet."

Nervously chuckled my colleague Phil in his Northern drone.

"Ha, ha, ha . . . I didn't mean to get you with the CS. You got in the way just as it was too late. I got him in the end though."

I had been in receipt of a full on squirt of the stuff, but I was relieved not to be blinded for life and readily accepted Phil's apology, reminding him of his attack on me from time to time, when I was in need of a favour.

One of the most rewarding jobs is being called to a report of a Concern for Safety, where, for example someone hasn't been seen for some time. I'd arrive and try various methods of getting into the home, which at times meant smashing a window with the use of the truncheon and climbing though.

I'd sometimes find myself saving a vulnerable elderly person who was collapsed on the floor within and be scooping them up to be taken to hospital. Other times I'd arrive to find they were no longer of this earth and have to deal with the call as a Sudden Death. I am of the belief that the person's spirit may still be around for a while, so I'd ensure I dealt with their remaining shell with all the dignity and respect that I could, regardless of who or what they may have been.

At times, once I was sure there had been no foul play, I'd find myself clearing away bloody sheets, congealed buckets of blood and the slimy remains where rotten flesh had been removed by the undertakers. I did this in an attempt to protect relatives from further distress and of course assure them that their loved one had appeared to have died peacefully.

During my probationary period, I had to visit the mortuary to watch a post-mortem. We were warned against the smell and offered an odour gel to put under our noses. I declined this offer as I didn't want to give the impression that I was some weak willed WPC, not up to the task in hand. I shut off my nose and concentrated on breathing through my mouth. The examination room where we stood was metallic and clinical, with a waxwork looking figure laid before us. I watched as the body was cut open and various internal organs shown to us and some removed. Over the years, my memories of this post mortem have been contaminated by what I've seen in films, but what I do recall from that day was the bright orange colour of the fat globules under the skin. I remember the head being cut so that the face could be pulled back to reveal the brain and growth gland, which has its very own compartment in the skull. Bundles of blue tissue were used to fill in the head and torso, before everything was pulled and sewn back into place. It was explained that this body would be having a bit of a make-over, with a wash and blow dry, perhaps with the help of a few rollers and a bit of make-up, before leaving the mortuary suite.

Over time, I developed the art of closing off the nostrils to breathe through the mouth. There would be many a time when I'd go into homes that smelt highly offensive. For me, the biggest offender of smells is damp dog. This particular odour is usually mixed with the stench of stale cheap tobacco, a dash of vomit, urine, rodent and a huge splash of eau-de-repulsive body odour. If the home reeked like that then the occupants would never smell of roses. With this smell came the most unhygienic surroundings, with rotten food, faeces, empty alcohol containers, overflowing ash trays and piles upon piles of dirty damp clothing around a thread bare mattress on the floor. The obligatory adapted crack pipe, tin foil, bent spoons and used syringes would of course be there for good measure. I'd be sure to touch the lift buttons with my knuckles, rather than finger tips and never eat a sandwich until I'd had a good hand scrub.

With less than three years into my police service, I was a well respected member of the shift and was offered various courses. Following my training at Hounslow, I became a

Level 2 Shield Trained Officer, called out to attend various major public order events in London. The training was tough, having wooden bricks, car tyres and petrol bombs lobbed at me. I accepted this course because I was a young, keen officer, intent on getting as many feathers in my cap as I could. The whole All Action Hero thing was not really fitting to my character. However, as a Sexual Offences Investigative Techniques (S.O.I.T) Officer, I excelled.

If the division had a serious sexual offence allegation on their hands, then the DS was keen to get me as the S.O.I.T. Much has improved with the law, procedures and facilities since my time in this role. In those days, video interviewing was not common place and my task was to get lengthy hand written statements from victims of rape, which would include details of the victims past history. It would not be unusual for these statements to consist of more than fifty pages. That didn't include the pages upon pages of written notes that I'd make before the actual statement writing could begin. For me, being a S.O.I.T officer involved a hundred percent commitment and dedication. Unfortunately whilst undertaking this position, I also quickly learnt the appalling truth, that some women lie about being raped, for a house move or some other personal benefit or gain. However, it has been a privilege to have met some truly brave inspirational victims of such a horrific intrusive crime.

I spent over a year as a Domestic Violence Officer. I'd meet those victims who upon first glance appeared absolutely fine, yet as they peeled back their sleeves, lifted their top or let me feel their head, they'd be black and blue; their attackers would beat them on the parts of their bodies where it wouldn't be readily seen. It wasn't all bad though, because apparently after the initial punch or kick you don't feel the rest of the beating. Some would explain that the love of their life first attacked them when they were pregnant, but they remained with him because he had promised that he really would change this time. Some had never been physically attacked at all. They'd be the ones checking their watches because they couldn't be out for too long; their partner was keeping a time check and would accuse them of seeing someone else. They would be the ones who'd have it drummed into them that they were fat, ugly and that no one else would ever be interested in them. They were the victims who had no control over their finances and felt trapped in the unfulfilling relationship.

These victims came from all walks of life, although my main customers were those who were unemployed or in menial employment. Not because there was more likelihood that they'd be victims or offenders, but because a criminal record for a solicitor or police officer would turn the lives of their whole family upside down. Job losses would be likely to follow, which would not be in the interests of all concerned, so would remain unreported, undetected and be a dirty little secret within the family home.

About four years into my police service I experienced a major knock in my confidence, which is something I continue to manage to this day. I recall it being an unremarkable day, doing unremarkable, none threatening tasks. I was out with PC Tommy Stone, chatting about our future aspirations; his to emigrate to Australia and mine to move to the country. Tommy and I were taking it in turns to stop cars. I did my usual of standing behind the tree waiting for the cheeky no right turn . . . But this time it all felt so different. My capture was a pleasant lady in her late twenties to early thirties with a couple of young kids in the back of the car. She was apologetic about her mister-meaner and I set about going through the verbal spiel of how she could accept the fine and penalty points to avoid court. I began writing the ticket and found my hands frantically shaking. I struggled to fit the letters and characters into the boxes on the form, but had to persevere to save face. Tommy was standing nearby to see me filling out the ticket, but thankfully not close enough to see my shaking hands or my heart pounding at a rate of knots. This ticket took me ages to write and I have no idea how I ever managed to complete it, nor what I ever did with this crumpled piece of paper. However, what I do know is that it changed the way I operated. I found that I began to avoid giving out tickets in case I replicated this response again. Without warning the same thing happened again, but this time it was when I was taking fingerprints. After that episode, I would make various excuses or volunteer for an alternative task so as to avoid fingerprinting.

I read self help books and tried the techniques of calm thoughts, but none of this worked; you see, I never knew when I was to get an anxiety attack as they had a habit of coming over me at times when there was no reason to feel anxious. I was still able to talk, walk and breathe as if nothing was wrong, so I was able to hide the attacks, appearing more confident and controlled than ever. At court, I'd place my report on the table in front of me and tuck my arms smartly behind my back, so that the excessive hand shaking was concealed.

If I was eating or drinking around colleagues and had an anxiety attack, then I'd quickly take my cup with both hands and gulp down my drink whilst they were looking away. I'd do the same with my meals, avoiding using a knife and folk at the same time. Instead I'd scoop the food quickly into my mouth with the cutlery in my stronger right hand. Perhaps I'd say was no longer hungry. I must explain that for most of the time I was absolutely fine and had no anxiety at all. However, it always remained in the back of my mind that this thing could grip me at any time.

I didn't know my GP and he didn't know me, but I went along to the surgery and explained my plight. He seemed rather unsympathetic and disinterested as I confessed that the anxiety attacks were causing me to question my ability to continue with my career. I was prescribed Propranalol. They were little pink 10mg tablets that I was instructed to take three times a day. I took these without fail. Although they seemed to take the edge off the feeling I had, my hands would still shake without warning and I continued to avoid fingerprints and tickets. I remained confident to deal with confrontation and hostile situations as they had not yet brought on that unwanted surge of excessive adrenalin.

I confided in Neil about my anxiety attacks and the medication I was taking, telling him how I felt embarrassed about my uncontrollable reactions to situations and that I was failing myself in some way. I stressed that I had managed to conceal this from others and wanted to keep it that way. However, just sometimes, Neil would say something, at a dinner party with friends perhaps and make a subtle mention about the little pink tablets. He'd then get a *"please don't say anything"* glare from me and I'd spend the rest of the time fearing my secret was about to be revealed. I don't know why he would do that, but he just did that, sometimes.

It took over five years for the house prices to creep up enough for us to sell our home at the same price we'd bought it for. By now I was frustrated with London living. What had been an exciting hustle and bustle was now a claustrophobic irritation of an overcrowded impersonal existence. I was tired of clubbing it and loathed the battle of the shopping trolleys at my local Tesco. I began to despise living in London and if I thought about it too much I felt like I couldn't breathe.

Whenever possible, we'd go for weekends down South to visit my family. I realised that we could have a wonderful home and lifestyle if we were to escape London and move away. For many people, their employment would restrict them, however, we had the option of applying to transfer to another police force.

I was aware that a transfer to another force was likely to include a stringent interview and fitness test. Failure was not an option and I set about going for five mile daily runs before work and going even further during the weekends. After jumping through quite a few hoops, Neil and I were successful in the interview and accepted for a force transfer. I was to swap my chequered cravat for a black tie and join the Constabulary. We had some savings which we first thought we'd have to use to get out of negative equity. However, we had a result because we managed to sell the house for the same price we'd paid for the property five years earlier. It was a big move in both home, location and career, but I felt we were good and ready for it.

Chapter Three

SHOW ME HEAVEN

"*WELL JACK, ERRH, THE reason we've taken you out for dinner tonight, is errh, well, me and Michelle want to get married . . . if it's okay with you?*"

This was Neil's moment when asking my dad's permission for my hand in marriage. Although we'd known one another for just twelve months, this proposal came of no great surprise. Nan and Dad had been making less than subtle suggestions about it since Neil and I had moved in together. I got the impression that they felt our actions of being shacked up together immoral out of wedlock. My father would question me,

"*What are your intentions with Neil? Are you both in love? You don't want to end up a second hand rose.*"

I would have loved to have been able to say to Dad,

"*Well, he is a guy who I love at the moment and we're going to see how we get on and if it works. If not, then we'll go our separate ways.*"

However, that type of mindset was not encouraged by my family.

The following year, Neil and I had the offer of a discounted dream holiday. It was an opportunity we didn't want to miss out on, but it seemed a rather extravagant vacation and more suited as a honeymoon. This was the final push for us to get married and we set a date for later that same year.

My parents became the wedding planners as we lived in London and their home town was the more suitable wedding location. I do not recall having very much involvement in deciding the venue or meal choice, but they were paying and had previous experience in such things, so I was content to leave them to it.

I set about putting my calligraphy skills to use by hand writing the wedding invitations. With the help of the Argos catalogue, I included a gift list, which consisted of,

Spring Bouquet bread and pedal bins
Philips steam iron
M&S peach coloured towel set
Plastic coated apron
Floral bordered mirror
Vogue Elegance cutlery set
Hollow fibre pillows and stretch fitted sheets
Heritage four piece oven to tableware set
Contributions towards a luggage set

I borrowed my wedding dress, which in its time was an up to date, full on meringue, complete with frills and bows. I made my little sisters bridesmaids dresses and gathered up dried flowers, nuts, corn and fir cones for the church and table decorations. I set these in baskets around the venues, then gave them out as gifts at the end of the event.

A quaint little church on the outskirts of town beside beautiful grounds was the wedding location. Our guests squeezed into the tiny old building to sing Lord of the Dance and Jerusalem, with the assistance of a choir. A small family run hotel was hired out to entertain and accommodate everyone at the reception that followed. The guests were greeted at The Wedding Breakfast with a glass of sherry. Vegetable soup was the starter, followed by a roast beef meal and a Black Forest Gateau for dessert. The evening buffet was plentiful, with a grand selection of bridge rolls, fingers of pizza, cocktail sausage rolls, cheese and pineapple sticks, Scotch eggs, quiche and that 90's buffet must have of creamed chicken and mushroom vol-au-vents. This wasn't just any buffet food, this was proper pucker party food!

Our first dance that day was Maria Mckee's, Show Me Heaven. I was sure I'd already seen heaven as the whole day had gone like a dream and many said it was the best wedding ever! I felt like I had the prize catch. We put out a wedding book for guests to sign and for us to add our hopes for the future, which read;

To live in a big house in North London with lots of money to spend on clothes, holidays and pine furniture. To be able to afford to buy all our weekly shopping from Marks and Spencer's.

Don't be too surprised about the shallowness of the above, not forgetting that they were the aspirations of a twenty-one year old newly wed. Following on from the honeymoon I was now proudly known as Mrs Charles. On reflection, I think that part of the attraction to marriage was an affirmation that I was all grown up and to be taken seriously.

Neil and I often worked conflicting shift patterns; being young and living close to the centre of London, we were keen to party with friends, but sometimes had to do this without one another. I'd go out with my mates and he'd go out with his. We'd dance the night away at places like Faces in Ilford, Hombres off Oxford Street or one of the many 999 Discos or section house parties.

These were the days of spiral perms, big curly hair and dungarees. I'd never be daring enough for the hot pants. It was only after one of my many diets when I'd lost weight, was fit and looking really good, that I slid easily into a gorgeous pair of Olivia Newton John (In Grease) style tight black shiny trousers. I found that in my twenties, when I set my mind to a fitness regime or weight loss programme, then I would be successful. However, I'd relapse and go through the same thing twelve months later. I loved experimenting with cooking, making big dishes of flap-jacks, trifles and treacle pudding and at times ignored the heavy calorific value in such things.

I tried cheating with the weight loss, buying packets of laxatives which were disguised as little chunks of chocolate, but I found that after a short time my stomach became more resilient than ever and they stopped working. I tried and failed at Bulimia; my method was to eat lots of food, drink lots of water and fizzy drinks, jump up and down a lot, then stick my fingers down my throat. No matter how much I tried, I gagged and gagged, but could not progress to the actual vomiting stage. For my efforts, the food remained in me and my weight loss attempt on that occasion turned into a weight gain.

I joined slimming clubs, tried detoxifying liquids, water retention tablets, counted calories and signed up for a year long health club membership, only to make it to the gym on a handful of occasions. Through trial and error I learnt that the best way to manage my weight was to eat sensibly and do fitness training . . . Just as the text books tell us.

With my fluctuating weight came the desire to reinvent myself from time to time. I'd have long blonde hair, then decide it was time for a change and have it chopped short and dyed red or perhaps brown or black. I loved hair pieces and coloured contact lenses, nail extensions and temporary tattoos. It would be easy for anyone to think Neil had numerous different wives on the go with the number of image changes I put myself through.

We both wore wedding rings; Neil bragged that his had become quite a Chick Magnet. He remained as charming as ever with the ladies and I felt pride that my gorgeous husband was admired by other women. I was confident that he was all mine, so much so that I would never feel jealous of any attention he got from others. He'd sometimes forewarn me that there was some untrue rumour going around work about him, or that a female colleague had become infatuated with him, but that he had no interest in any other women.

"Why have a burger when I can have steak at home?" he'd assure me.

With all his charm and good looks, I could forgive a woman for taking an interest in him. Neil loved me and I adored him. I could see no reason why he'd ever want to stray from our marriage.

Having left London for the new country living, Neil was making friends and having new interests. Apparently, with this new location came a whole new set of gossipers; he'd report back to me that work colleagues had yet again decided to target him by spreading untruths. I had no reason to doubt Neil's account and couldn't see how he'd ever have the chance to have an illicit affair or three, because he'd simply have no time to do so. He was too busy going off for shooting or diving weekends, or visiting his parents in London. The idea of him having an affair would be ridiculous, if not impossible.

A couple of times a year we enjoyed some great holidays abroad together. For much of the time Neil was great company, but sometimes I didn't feel quite as loved as I'd hoped. During one ski holiday with work buddies, he practically ignored me and we had a huge embarrassing bust up where I felt humiliated in front of the group. He was so remorseful about his despicable behaviour, describing me as his lovely, caring, beautiful wife and vowed to treat me like a Princess in the future.

Neil was a wonderful brother-in-law to Abigail and Natasha, who'd grown up with him around. He'd take them to the Zoo, arrange visits to see the police horses and we'd go away on trips with them to Disneyland. The little girls adored him. My dad considered Neil to be his best mate. They shared an interest in shooting, would wear matching club sweaters and go on trips together. As for Mum, well she would see good in everyone and be a friend to all.

Neil could be very selfish. He'd spend his money on extravagant items for himself, run into debt, then I'd bail him out. When I was feeling low with a back injury, he simply wasn't around to help me. By now we had a dog and I needed to take the pet for daily walks and had to struggle with pain to do this alone, as Neil had gone away on yet another trip.

For most of the time, our relationship seemed one that was made in Heaven, but as the cracks started to appear, Heaven didn't seem quite the same as it had in earlier years.

Something was wrong and I couldn't put my finger on what it was. I should have been so happy, yet there was a discontentment eating away inside of me. I would stand in front of the mirror crying, questioning my unsettled feelings with such guilt. I blamed myself for this feeling, thinking that perhaps I was unhappy because I'd joined the job far too young, and become grown up and sensible far to soon.

I was in my late twenties with a big house, apparently settled lifestyle, so there was an expectation that the next step would be children. I definitely wanted to have a family, yet felt I needed to do more with my life before taking that leap. I spoke to Neil about my feelings and suggested to him that I should take a career break to see a bit of the world. If we were to sell our home and buy something a little smaller, then we could cope on one wage. Surprisingly, Neil seemed quite supportive of my idea to have time out to travel, saying he loved me and wanted whatever was going to make me happy. He seemed a little too keen to have me go away for a while. Something about his support, together with my feelings of discontentment, suggested to me that things were not quite right with our relationship.

CHAPTER FOUR

ALL CRIED OUT

THE BIG FAT QUESTION . . . How does one work out if their husband is having an affair?

My sub consciousness was telling me that something wasn't right within our relationship. Neil had asked me if I was having an affair and questioned if I was true to him. I noticed he had new expensive trendy branded clothing, which he claimed he'd snapped up for a bargain price in yet another sale or that he'd had it for ages. He had a pager which he was secretive about and spoke of needing a mobile phone. There were times when he'd be rather demanding for sex, yet he'd recently lost interest in intimacy with me. Friends were starting to act oddly in our company, as if they knew something I didn't. He would often talk excitedly about some random female he'd met at work with an over enthusiastic interest. He had some scratch marks on his back and claimed he'd fallen in a thorn bush during a shift.

I asked him directly if he was having an affair and he fervently denied it, claiming I was paranoid and stupid to think such a thing. I had a friend who was having an affair with a married man, but few of my friends were married and none had knowingly been cheated on. So, I had no one to seek advice from. I thought about things I'd seen about this subject on television or at work and set about conducting my own private investigation.

Now, on TV I'd seen women checking their husbands shirt collars for the smell of unfamiliar perfume or a smudge of lipstick and checking through trouser and jacket pockets for clues. So, the laundry basket was where I started.

Over the course of about a week, I dug through the dirty washing, sniffing collars and fishing through pockets. There was no lipstick or perfume, but I found two receipts. One was from Currys for £99.99. There was nothing on this to say what the item was that had been purchased, but there was a product code and the store telephone number. I phoned Currys. I explained that I was checking through my receipts and questioned what this one was for. Within moments they were able to confirm this was for a Sanyo Hi-Fi system, which there was no sign of in our home. Another receipt clearly showed a very recent purchase of a set of £20 hair clippers, which we had no need for as the old ones were working just fine.

I checked through his drawers and scrawls in his work diary. I found a business card for a PC Suzie Blue of Essex Police. I didn't know where she fitted in within my investigation, but I retained this as evidence just in case. I found a bank statement from the previous year which had two payments for two separate florist shops on the same day. I couldn't work out why this would be the case. If you need flowers, then why not purchase them from the same shop?

I sorted out our household bills, including the phone bill, which was never itemised. I called BT and they agreed to send me back dated itemised bills. I kept a watchful eye to be first to catch the morning post and within days the paperwork arrived. Once alone, I set about checking through. I noticed that the number 123 was dialled frequently and couldn't think why. I checked my diary and the shifts I'd been on and saw the phone would be used within minutes of me walking out of the door for work.

A week later I confronted Neil about my findings. I was confused, angry and tearful, yet he was calm and calculated, giving an explanation for my findings. The clippers and Hi-Fi were for one of his diving buddies who asked him to get the items, then repaid him. There was a bit of a delay, but I eventually clicked that 123 was for the speaking clock. Why would he want to dial that when we had plenty of clocks around the house and there was a charge for this call? Neil explained that he simply wanted to make sure he kept his wrist watch accurate in time. The use of separate florists was accounted for as he'd ordered flowers for me in the morning and by the afternoon he was walking past another florist when he decided to send flowers to his mother. I was therefore misinterpreting his kindness and thoughtfulness with my psycho paranoid thoughts. I was advised to end such a ridiculous mindset as it was wrong for me to distrust him.

The problem for Neil was that I couldn't end my thoughts. I just couldn't let it rest. I stopped asking him about my findings as he was getting more and more angry by this. There was one particular number that kept featuring in the itemised bill and showed up as the number dialled before the speaking clock. I questioned Neil about this and even suggested that I call it. He was adamant that I must not do this under any circumstances. He claimed that this was actually the number of a very important police informant and if I was to call the number I'd ruin everything and put his job and mine on the line.

I decided I had to face this head on. I scribbled down the number and the following evening whilst Neil was watching TV, I claimed I needed to go to the local corner shop for some milk. I left the house and walked to the phone box. As I walked along the busy street, I could see the little cubicle illuminated, glowing like a bright beacon of final destination. My breathing became laboured and my heart was thumping like a deep heavy drum. I pulled back the kiosk door to the distinctive smell of urine and cigarettes. The heavy metal framed door closed itself. I felt safe in the privacy of this glass box. I pulled out the crumpled number and began dialling it. It was a local number. I stopped and cancelled my call. My hands now clammy and shaking. How was I to start my conversation with whoever was to answer at the other end? Would anyone answer? What if it was an important police informant and I was about to betray their confidentiality? I had to do this, so here goes . . . Ring ring . . .

"Hello" said the chirpy, childlike sounding female on the other end of the line.

"Hello, I'm not sure how to start this call, but my name is Michelle Charles and I think you might know my husband,"

"Oh, okay, yes. I've been expecting your call." This strangers voice sounded kind and understanding, so I continued on.

"I think my husband is having an affair and I've been checking my phone bill and see that your number features on it a lot."

Penny explained that she had been seeing Neil for nearly two years. As she went into more details, I was doing the calculations in my head. Two years!? We moved from London nearly two years ago, so the affair must have started almost immediately after our move.

Penny told me that Neil had brought her back to our home, shown her our individual bedrooms (he claimed our floral guestroom was my bedroom) and said we lived separate lives, but kept up the pretence of being together to appease my parents. This was all of course untrue and I updated Penny on this. We had so many questions for one another, so arranged a time to meet and ended the call.

I felt such relief. I'd just had a confirmation that I wasn't going mad and that my suspicions were indeed credible. I do not recall my walk back home, nor what followed when I set eyes on Neil after that call. Not surprisingly, Neil had already been on the phone to Penny and was now fully aware that he'd been exposed as a cheating, selfish, deceitful, lying wanker! He gathered up a few bits in a holdall and I ordered him out of the house.

The following days are something of a blur. I'd sip on red wine but couldn't get rid of a foul taste in my mouth and had no interest in eating. My body trembled and I had the involuntary shaking of my left leg, then my right. I would sob myself to sleep and wake with the realisation that the affair was still reality and that I'd only been asleep for a short time. I was hovering on the need to be hysterical, yet had too little energy through being so emotionally drained. I was full of self doubt, questioning if it was in fact my actions, behaviour and possible neglect that had pushed my husband into the arms of another woman. I sat sobbing alone in the lounge, lit only by a couple of candles, whilst going through my CD collection playing songs I'd never really listened to before. For the first time ever I could hear and fully understand the lyrics thumping through the room and travelling into the heart and soul of my being. The power and passion of those sounds and words was electrifying and whilst the songs pumped through my veins I could breathe and feel such a release of emotions.

Lenny Kravitz was there in the room with me . . . *"Siiisterrrr, did you have to fall in love, with a man, that never was . . . up to no good. He took your soul and he stole your only heart, flipped your wings and left a permanent scar . . ."*

Alison Moyet came in . . . *"All cried out! You took a whole lot of loving for a handful of nothing . . . take back your cold and empty heart!"*

By day, I knew I needed to get out of the house. I'd walk as if in a bubble, oblivious to my surroundings, consumed by the torment of being lied to for so long. I didn't want to see anyone I knew. I had no idea what I'd say to them and wasn't sure I even had the energy to utter the words. Inside I felt I was dying and didn't care about anything anymore.

Neil returned to the house. He looked so different with his new crew cut. He looked older, tired and drained. He looked empty inside. The Neil I'd previously known and adored had gone and could never come back again. An ugly shell of betrayal was now standing before me. The twisted torment for me was that it felt like a bereavement. The person who I had adored had died in my heart. But ironically they had never really existed in the first place. Now that the repulsive truth was out, I asked if there were any other lies. I needed to know the full truth, no matter how bad it was, so as to end my suffering. He was aware I was visiting Penny and claimed that I now knew everything.

What was I to wear to meet the other woman? I tried on various outfits and finally picked a plain short sleeved black top and black trousers. The trousers were usually a little tight, but were now hanging loosely on me. I selected cubic zirconia stud earrings and a matching necklace. I wore black ankle boots with a slight heel and put on just a little bit of make-up.

I got the directions to Penny's from Neil, after all, he'd been there enough times. It was about a ten minute drive away and en route I stopped to have a cigarette and apply some lip gloss. As I drove into Penny's road, children were out in the street, running around and kicking a ball. I was a little concerned about parking my car there for fear of some accidental damage. I nervously knocked on the door and was somewhat taken aback by the figure standing before me.

Penny was petite and about five inches shorter than me. She was pretty, with short impish styled blonde hair. She was about five years older than me and had quite a hardened face. She invited me into her small home, which felt welcoming and familiar. As I scanned around, I noticed that we shared a similar style of décor. This may have been something to do with the general styles and fashions of that time, but there were lots of things alike to those in my home. The Chinese style rugs, pine furniture, stencil boarders and even the kitchen curtains with the chicken print design, exactly the same as mine.

She made me a cup of tea in the same style mug I had at home. I was a Marlborough Light smoker, but accepted one of hers, from a packet of Blue Berkley. Neil had recently started smoking this brand. We smoked, drank tea and talked and talked. The hours passed as we shared the lies we'd both been told and filled each other in on the facts to rewrite the fiction. I was grateful for Penny's honesty as she willingly answered the most intrusive of questions, all of which I needed the answers to in order to combat my inner anguish.

A big smack in the face for me was when she produced a photo of her and Neil together. It was just like one of the many happy couple photos I had at home, but Penny was in this one, not me. I suggested to Penny that her and Neil could continue a relationship together as I had no interest in him anymore, but her response to that was,

"I don't want him now. He can get lost."

A couple of hours into my visit, Neil turned up at Penny's door to return her door key and more than likely check on us both. By now her children had returned home and were excited by Neil's arrival.

"I love you Neil," said the youngest.

I closed my eyes and took a deep breath, feeling anger and concern. Not only had Neil messed with mine and Penny's heads by his selfish actions, but he was playing with tiny innocent hearts that clearly adored him. The children would be devastated if he was to suddenly disappear from their world.

Neil had painted a truly awful picture of me to Penny consisting of blatant lies. He'd told her that he really wanted a family and was therefore happy to be around her children. He claimed that I did not want children and had even had an abortion without his consent. All of this was of course untrue. I'd never even been pregnant.

He'd lied to Penny that he had numerous talents, roles in his job and experiences that only just fell short of him being a real life James Bond. By the end of the evening we were exhausted from the exchange of truths and I had no wish to return home. Penny gave me a night shirt and by the early hours I was laying with her in her bed, the side where Neil had laid on many occasions. I turned myself on my side, placed a wad of tissues at the top of my cheek against the pillow and cried myself to sleep for yet another night.

Penny was never my enemy. She had made no commitment to me, had broken no marriage vows, nor told any untruths. Over a short time we'd formed an alliance and had a common bond as we had both been cheated by Neil. His work colleagues knew about Penny as she'd met most of them at various functions. How humiliating for me, as everyone must have been aware of Neil's cheating and I was the last to find out. With this new knowledge I didn't know who I could now trust. Penny came up with an idea. We got glammed up and went out into town. She knew the various places where Neil's associates would be, propping up some bar. Penny and I confidently strutted into the popular pub, arm in arm and I'm sure Neil's friends nearly choked on their pints as they clearly knew who we both were and were understandably shocked by our apparent friendship.

My family were completely against my association with Penny, telling me that it was a strange set up and that I must be crazy. They encouraged me to continue my marriage with Neil, saying that he was truly sorry and that I had probably brought about his infidelity, by my obsession with getting the house renovated and wanting everything done yesterday.

"Look what you'd be giving up, this big house, lovely garden. All the hard work that's been put in to it would be a waste."

"If you want a divorce then we consider this to be a breach of contract and would be looking to be reimbursed by you for the money we paid towards your wedding."

"Everyone thinks you're weird Michelle and mad for associating with that Penny woman."

Despite these protests, I felt empowered in Penny's company and we began socialising together and introducing one another to our friends. She became 'my friend Penny'. She had such endearing qualities. Yes, she was rough around the edges, taking me to some of the shabbiest of pubs and directing me to stub my cigarette out on the carpet, as these drinking establishment had no ashtrays. She was flirtatious with the men and spoke to them with cheeky innuendo. She would scan around the pubs and clubs that we frequented, spotting the guys with the fattest wallets, then befriend them for long enough to get our drinks paid for, making it a very cheap night.

She became my co-investigator and together we scanned through our diaries, through the itemised phone bills and recalled previous conversations Neil had had with us. We were absolutely sure he'd lied to us both. It appeared there had been other women involved in his sordid life and he'd gone to great lengths to live this gigolo lifestyle, in what must have been thirty-six hour days. I phoned Suzie Blue and she confirmed what I'd anticipated. We established the use of separate florists on the same day was to hide his affair from the shopkeeper, sending flowers declaring his love to Penny and a separate bunch with a similar message to me.

123 was indeed the speaking clock. If I was to have pressed last number redial, then that's what I'd dial rather than Penny's number. We established there had been numerous other women and that Neil had been untrue to me from the very start of our relationship. I confronted him about my findings to be told yet more lies, which made it impossible for me to remove my ongoing inner suffering.

After all these devastating discoveries, I tried desperately to keep my marriage together to please my family and even went to marriage guidance counselling. Neil and I continued living in our home and my friend Penny and her kids would visit us. Neil would smother me with his affections, promise that he was a changed man and that we'd be together forever. At times I'd believe him, but as I uncovered yet another lie, distrust returned and we were back to square one.

With the discovery that he had been having sex with multiple partners for years, the concern for me was that I may have a sexually transmitted infection. Neil was given no choice in the matter as I instructed that we go to the GUM Clinic at the hospital. It was so humiliating to be in that waiting room, dreading that I was going to be seen by someone I knew.

We were individually seen by a nurse for samples to be taken. They asked why I had come to the clinic and I explained it was due to my husband shagging around. They advised me that their early tests showed I had Chlamydia, which if untreated could cause infertility. I was not told how long I was likely to have had this condition, but given a short course of antibiotics, and with our own individual boxes of medication we were sent on our way.

I felt pressured by both my family and by Neil to remain in this marriage and could see no easy way out without a lot of disruption for all. My feelings remained that I needed to do something with my life and see the world before having children. Neil was willing to support me in this on the understanding that we would remain very much together. Although I was going away, he'd be able to go on an extended holiday to visit me. It would not be unlike a soldier or sailor having to leave his family whilst on tour. I applied for a one year work permit for Australia, as I felt this would be a safe destination for a lone female traveller like myself, and my parents had friends I could stay with there. My Visa application and planning for this trip was a welcome distraction. We worked out that we'd be able to keep our home with just Neil's wage as he vowed to stop his selfish wasteful spending on toys for himself.

By the Summer, I had the confirmation that my Visa application was successful. My career break had been granted and I set the date and booked my flight to Perth.

Then came the unexpected call from Tommy Stone. I'd not heard from him for about three years and had not kept in touch with him since he left the job and emigrated. He explained that he was back in the UK for a few months and noticed I was no longer working in London. He'd managed to find me through the Constabulary and suggested we meet up. A week later, he came to visit and told me all about his new life in Perth, suggesting I contact him once I get there as he could introduce me to his friends and see I was okay. At this point I think it's worth me explaining that there was never any possible love interest here. Tommy was attractive enough, being well built, blonde. He had an endearing laid back attitude, but he was nearly twenty years my senior and had daughters closer to my age. I identified him to be more of an Uncle figure than anything else.

The weeks before my departure were difficult ones of mixed emotions, still uncovering lies. Neil's moods were terrible with him saying I was winding him up then punching his head or the floor. He'd damage things and I'd set about concealing the hole in the door or the smashed light switch.

I was angry with his display of affection, when sending me a huge bunch of flowers at my place of work, as if to prove something to everyone else, rather than to me. I searched for answers to my future from Tarot Cards, which I initially had little faith in. That was until the reader who had never met me, spoke of my planned Australia travels and identified Neil with the use of the Trickster-Magician card, saying he was not all that he appeared to be.

The day I left was chilly and foggy. Neil and I stayed overnight at a Heathrow Hotel as I had an early morning flight. Once at the airport, we went into a photo booth to have our picture taken together. It was an emotional goodbye with tears streaming down our faces as we hugged and kissed at the departure gate. This was to be our very last physical contact with one another. As I walked through the departure gate, losing sight of Neil, a transformation was occurring, with a voice inside my head from Stars In Their Eyes saying,

"Tonight Matthew, I'm going to be myself, I'm going to finally be Michelle."

This was the start of a new chapter in my life and I really needed this.

CHAPTER FIVE

MAN IT'S A HOT ONE

THE BLUEST OF SKY, brightest of sunshine and most persistent of flies, which were intent on plunging into every available body orifice. This was Spring in Perth, Western Australia, and I loved it!

The day after my arrival I phoned Tommy,

"Hey! so you made it here okay," exclaimed Tommy.
"I've been expecting your call. I'm off to a party tonight and it would great if you can come with me. I've told all my friends that you're a wild crazy chick!"

It took about forty minutes by train to get to Tommy's place. He picked me up from the station and we went for a drive. With windows open to give some relief from the heat, Santana's Smooth was blaring out from the car radio. We travelled along the Great Western Highway coastal drive, passed the palm tree lined sandy beaches. This was just so cool! Tommy drove me up to Kings Park, with its entrance of willowy white ghost gum trees and breathtaking views of the city. Flocking from tree tops, I was amazed to see brilliant red and green birds. They looked as if they'd escaped from a cage. We drove through the network of roads, crossing this beautiful park as Tommy pointed out the little plaques beside each tree, in memory of one of the many who died in the world wars. The numbers on these memorials flashed in front of my eyes,

22, 19, 21, 27, 18, 18 . . .

This was indeed a whack across the knuckles. A stark reality check, that life is so precious. That no matter how bad things had been for me recently and how sorry I'd felt for myself, I was still living and breathing at the age of twenty-eight, so every day was a bonus and I should make the most of it.

We went on to the party. I had to forget my jet lag because the pressure was on and an expectation set. Those party goers were expecting the arrival of a crazy Pommy chick and I didn't want to disappoint, because I'd be letting Tommy down if I was to fall short of this.

I was on a life high. I'd left a dull Winter, arrived to a sizzling Summer and had nowhere in particular to be for the next year. It doesn't get much better than that! The party was buzzing with young enthusiastic people. One of Tommy's friends had his guitar and amplifier set up, and was keeping us mesmerised with his soulful voice. The drinks were flowing and everyone was keen to meet me. The surfer dude Luke, was the keenest and throughout the evening kept appearing at my side like a puppy dog. He was my height, if not a little bit shorter and nine years my junior. He had long blonde hair and the cheekiest of smiles that made his eyes light up. Although he was a scaffolder by day, he was a

G-string waiter by night. He told me that there was a market for skimpy waitresses and felt I'd be ideal for such a job.

By now I'd had quite a bit to drink, so with my inhibitions subdued, his job suggestion sounded very tempting. I had a possible full time job open to me in a chain of high street jewellers, but a skimpy waitress could earn at least five times more for a lot less work. I could see no point being on a career break if I needed to work long hours in an underpaid job. I was very tempted.

A couple of days later Tommy called me. He said that the puppy dog hadn't stopped talking about me and had arranged for me to meet a girl called Sadie who ran an agency for glamour waitresses. Luke had arranged for her to be at his place and she was expecting to meet me. So my drunken enthusiasm in this job had been taken seriously and Luke must have gone to a lot of trouble to get me this interview. I didn't want to let anyone down, it's not in my nature. What would I have to do in such an interview? Would Sadie have to examine my boobs for size and pertness? Was my bum too big? What about all my cellulite?

I put on my best red bra and knickers under a tight fitting combat style khaki top and trousers and Tommy dropped me off at Luke's home. He was sitting outside by the pool in the back yard, beside a wooden clad homemade bar. The coloured fairy lights illuminated an endless selection of spirit bottles in their optics; all empty of course. A pretty petite girl in heels teetered in. Her long sun kissed blonde wavy hair laid casually against the shoulders of her cutesy little dress. She stood confidently and upright with the most amazing figure. With a broad smile revealing the whitest of teeth she said,

"Hi Michelle, I'm Sadie. Pleased to meet you. Luke here has told me all about you."

Luke's puppy dog eyes lit up and I wondered what secrets I'd blurted out to him in my inebriated state a few days earlier. Sadie explained the job of a waitress. She advised never to stand with a hand on the hip slightly to the side, because that makes any girl look fat. Girls should stand upright with shoulders back and chest out to ensure that we look as gorgeous as possible. A golden rule was never to speak ill of the other girls, because it sounds bitchy and the guys don't like that. She said that many a time she'd turn up for a job and spend much of it buttering bread roles in just her G-string. But who cares, if you're still getting paid for it. Sadie reassured me that there were hard and fast rules of no touching of the girls and that money was to be paid up front by the clients. It was $45 an hour skimpy, which meant bra and g-string, $60 topless and $120 nude. She said that some of the girls chose not to do any nude work, which was fine. Sadie said her commission was just $10 for every hour booked. I listened intently to Sadie's words as I needed her crash course in a job I had absolutely no experience in. She didn't ask to look at my boobs, nor did she appear to be checking out my figure. She said she'd give me a call when she had a job for me.

Once Sadie left I confided in Luke that I was really nervous about the prospect of flashing my body off to strangers, although I didn't want to pull out of this job offer as the money was so good. Any regular job would pay me just $10 an hour. Luke invited me on a road trip later that week. He explained that a remote pub about three hours away had booked a G-string waiter and skimpy waitress. He suggested I could join them on that job to have a trial run of serving behind a bar. If I didn't feel confident enough when the time came then it didn't matter.

I bought myself my very first mobile phone. It was about six inches long, nearly an inch thick, with a two inch ridged protruding aerial. I started to get calls from a few people I'd met at the party as a network of friends was developing. One of my more frequent callers was the puppy dog. He'd call and say he was just passing on his way to a job. He lived nowhere near where I was staying but in the following weeks I spent a lot of time in his company.

Luke was a young enthusiastic guy who had recently moved from his mother's home and spent most of his money on his pride and joy, a large white Holden Commodore car, which he believed was the fastest on the road and envy of the town. It didn't impress me, but then cars never have; I just want them to get me from A to B.

Luke would give me a call, pick me up then we'd speed off down the highway on one of our many adventures. We'd have a few UDL cans and perhaps stop off at a remote winery to pick up a bottle for the road. We'd smoke loads. Luke would roll himself up something a little stronger and we'd have rock music thumping full blast as the Holden was driven as fast as it would allow, all the time looking to dodge the speed cameras and cop cars. He was thriving at being my little tour guide. He drove me down south to Albany, to the rocks with their blow holes and to the most beautiful of secluded beaches, with the finest white sands and brilliant sparkling aqua waters.

By now I was the thrill seeker, being taken to the Gloucester Tree in Pemberton. A flutter of nervousness engulfed me as I looked up at this two-hundred foot high giant, pegged with a spiral ladder to the very top. Luke passed me his joint and I inhaled a couple of deep crackly drags, then practically coughed my lungs up, struggling to catch my breath but ready to start my assent. Far enough up to be committed, I got a furious leg shaking attack. There was no safety net, nor a soft landing. If I was to lose my grip or footing then I'd be a gonner. Luke was following on behind, offering encouragement and reassurance. At the very top was the most breathtaking of panoramic views of the Karri Forest, with its crooked leafy branches and immense tranquillity. Some of the trees had dead branches clinging to their tops. One such tree had a lumpy bare head with Medusa looking branches swirling from it. I pointed out this resembling Mythical Goddess in search for its name.

"Is it the character from Scooby Doo?" enquired Luke

With that, the cannabis had clearly taken hold and I fell into a fit of uncontrollable giggles, reminded that Luke was so very young and I adored his innocence. I didn't care that my puppy dog was more than likely too stoned and under the influence for driving. I was living for the moment, having the most amazing care free time and I knew it would eventually end, so was going to savour every last drop.

About three hours drive south from Perth was a remote chicken farming settlement. This is where Luke had his next waiting job and where I was accompanying him for my practice run. The concept of standing behind a bar flashing off most of my lumpy arse in underwear seemed utterly bizarre. I struggled to understand why anyone would pay for such a service. But they did and I had to get my head around it.

I chose a more comical spin and made myself some furry animal print ears attached to a head band, put a feathery boarder around the top of my bra and attached a long wavy tail to the back of my thong . . . it even had a bell attached to the end! Luke was right, even with very little clothing, once I had my footwear on, I'd cheat a mindset of being suitably dressed.

So there I was, standing behind the bar in a crowded pub in my skimpy fancy dress costume, telling the guys that I was the 'Pussy' for the night. I'd never struggled with the Aussie accent up until now, when drinks orders were given in what sounded like a code. The local Emu Bitter and the popular Victoria Bitter would be ordered by the half pint as either a

"Middy of V.B," or
"Middy of E.B,"

both sounding exactly the same, yet apparently tasting completely different. Glasses were chilled and when handled should be done so by the middle as no one wants the servers fingers around the rim. A centimetre of head was desirable and if the pump didn't have enough gas, then some swirling and wanking of the glass might be required. If the customer was sitting at the bar, they'd place their money beside their glass, and once it was nearly empty the glass was to be refilled promptly. The skill here was to remember what the customers were drinking and once they finally turned their glass upside down, they were done and no more beer was served. If their glass was placed on its side then they'd want a 'Blue', which I was told was a fight. Thankfully I didn't see that. The money took some getting used to, with the tiny $2 coins filling the tills. The notes had a slightly plastic texture and brash bold colours, giving the impression of Monopoly Money.

My trial run was a success and the guys loved me. My confidence was sky high and I felt relieved that the experienced skimpy waitress was not as gorgeous as I'd anticipated. I got my normal clothes back on and joined the crowded pub with the jukebox spinning out my favourite tunes. I took centre stage on the dance floor and noticed the others mimicking my groovy dance moves. I was just so cool and for that night the Pommy chick had celebrity status!

I was given my first paying job as a Skimpy in Albany, which was about five hours drive from Perth. The Holden and puppy dog escorted me to the pub on the outskirts of town. As we rolled up to the venue a double sided black board was advertising me,

'Perth Skimpy, Here Tonight! 4-8'

The job came with paid expenses for fuel and they included the in-house accommodation, which was a tatty little room that hadn't seen a makeover for some twenty years. I popped on the ears and tail and once again I was Pussy. Luke looked admiringly at me, as if I was his creation and perhaps to some extent I was. I nervously stepped out behind the bar of this large pub to find just a handful of customers seated some distance away, seemingly disinterested by my arrival. The landlord gave me some brief instructions on how to work the till and where everything was, then the bar was down to me. My first customer asked for a C.C. and Dry, which threw me into confusion as I had no idea what this was. My little saviour Luke was in the wings and immediately came to the rescue, jumping behind the bar, directing me to the Canadian Club bottle and pointing out the mixers. A chubby man in his fifties propped himself and his money beside the bar and began fiddling with one of those little $2 coins.

"Do you flip?" he enquired.

I hadn't been aware of a requirement for acrobatics and gave him a puzzled stare. He immediately chuckled at my response,

"You're new to this game aren't you?"

Mr V.B. drinker then set about talking me through the rules of flipping,

"You're given a two dollar coin and toss it in the air. Heads I lose and you get to keep the two bucks, tails I win and you flash off ya tits . . . wanna have a try?"

There was no way I wanted to show my boobs off to this or any other man, not even a quick flash! I didn't have the plumpest of chests. Over the years from repeatedly dieting and jogging, the jelly bags had some what lost their stuffing. I wasn't ready for this yet and declined his offer. The shift remained relatively quiet and my wage probably cost the landlord more than his takings. That wasn't my problem, but I still felt a little disappointed by the apparent disinterest in me by the customers. It was such a contrast from a couple of days earlier. After an overnight stay we headed back to Perth the following morning.

Now that I'd just about secured a job, I needed a car. I'd set aside a budget of £1000 and hoped to get something half decent for that. However, I quickly established that second hand motors held their prices and the car lots didn't display anything less than $2000. Tommy suggested that nearby Cannington was the best location for car hunting, so that's where we headed. As we drove along the main strip, I was confronted with an endless stream of multi-coloured bunting flapping in the wind from the Freemantle Doctor, framing the unstylish rectangles of metal. Brashly displaying their worth with bold banners in the windscreen, proclaiming myths such as Good Runner, One lady Owner, Executive Model. I resigned myself to the fact that I had no idea whether I was getting ripped off or not, so placed my faith in Tommy's judgement. He'd been looking around to find me a suitable car and with the exchange of $2000 the deal was done.

I became the not so proud owner of a 1982 Honda Civic. It was white in colour, the sort of white that had been through the washing machine with a black sock lurking in the depths of the drum. The upholstery of the rear seats had long since melted in the heat of the many summers and was now flaking and peeled back to expose a discoloured foam. The radio struggled to tune into one crackly channel and the speedometer needle quivered so that I could never be quite sure of my exact speed.

I'd frequently be reminded that this car had no air conditioning. I'd foolishly open my drivers side window to the heat of a red hot oven blasting at the side of my face. I'd quickly close the window and try to convince myself that I was actually extremely lucky as I had my very own in-car sauna. Although there was nothing attractive about this car, it was my new companion, a tool in my independence and it was all mine. I was determined that we'd get along just fine.

It was inevitable that I'd be getting my boobs out for strangers, but I didn't know how to prepare myself for such an eventuality. I think that's why I was a bag of nerves at my first topless job from Sadie. I was directed out to the shed in the back yard. This was not some flimsy wooden tool shed that you'd find in a typical English back garden. This shed was something that resembled a full scale industrial unit, made of sturdy galvanised steel, complete with concrete floor, fitted lighting, pool table and TV. I later learnt that The Shed was an Aussie guys retreat. Women were usually only ever welcomed if they were delivering food and drink supplies or serving beer in very little clothing. I was casually welcomed for the latter. The host Ralphy, pointed to the corner,

"You'll find tinnies in blue eskie and the light beers and the premiums in the green one. Any problems let me know Doll."

Although I felt so very embarrassed and self conscious of my revealing appearance, the guys didn't seem that bothered, appearing to glance briefly at me, as if to say,

"Well I've seen ya tits, now get us a beer."

I was nothing unusual to them. It was common place for a group of guys to all chip in money, so as to buy some beers and snacks for a get together. They'd make sure enough cash was set aside to pay a toppo waitress to serve the beers. If they were really splashing out then they'd book a couple of waitresses, perhaps one from 6-8 and another from 7-9, then a stripper to entertain them with a half hour Fruit and Veg' or Vibrator and Bead Show. If they were going overboard then they'd book a finale of a Lesbian Strip Show. For that night, I was simply The Toppo.

Once again I donned the comedy ears and tail, but found this served only as a play thing, much to my annoyance. Around forty men were gathered, chatting together in small individual groups and as I went round talking briefly with each group, the tail would get yanked, pulling at the waistband of my g-string where it was attached, causing discomfort.

"Get the fuck off the tail!" is what I wanted to say,

But instead I smiled sweetly through gritted teeth and offered yet another beer. The priority for the guys was their beer. As long as it was cold, plentiful and served with a smile, then they were happy. There was no attempt to grab at me and although they sounded a little brash at times, I was among what appeared to be a group of nice enough guys who wanted me to feel comfortable in their company. If they sensed that I was uneasy or embarrassed by comments made by themselves or their mates, then they'd quickly back track and turn it around to make the guy who'd said something remotely offensive look a complete idiot.

With Christmas approaching, the holiday season was in full swing and the work came rolling in. I was the new girl and very much in demand. I don't doubt that I was being given many of the jobs that the experienced girls couldn't be doing with, like those further afield. However, at that time I was none the wiser and keen to grab the money whilst the work was plentiful. I'd work with other girls and they'd later phone with jobs they had for me. On reflection they were probably passing me on their pre-booked jobs as they'd been re-booked for better paying ones.

I got booked for a four hour topless job in a far out town called Collie, which was a three or four hour drive away. It seemed a long commute for a one off job, but the wages were enhanced, with travelling expenses and accommodation at a local hotel included. I took it as an opportunity to visit somewhere different, but didn't relish the thought of all that driving. Thankfully Caine volunteered to be my driver.

Caine was Luke's friend who I'd been introduced to at a barbeque. Although only a year or so older than Luke, he had a confident air about him, with his 6'4" muscular frame giving him a mature presence. He had a goaty beard, bleach blonde short spiky hair, with dark roots clearly visible and a thuggish brow piercing above his left eye. He had the scruffiest of cars, which he'd picked up for a steal and was keen to give it a good run.

So there I was, travelling off to my next job with a young guy I'd met for a matter of a few hours. He had a calm kindly voice and I melted as he ended his sentences to me with the word,

"Sweetie." (pronounced 'sweedie')

The nerves started to kick in as we approached the venue, down some dusty back road on an industrial estate out of town. Now that we'd sussed out where I was to be, we checked into the hotel, which was a room above a pub in town. It was once again a shabby looking pit stop, but was fit for purpose. I got changed into a little black party dress. Sadie advised that first impressions were important and girls should arrive at jobs well dressed, even though they wouldn't spend much time in the clothes. I got Caine to stop off at the drive-in bottle shop (off licence to you and I) and I picked up a couple of bottles of alco-pops, quickly swigging them down to ease my nerves.

"You'll be okay sweetie, I'll stick around," assured Caine.

I spent the following four hours in the hangar of a construction with around sixty men. I was the one and only female and probably the most attractive looking specimen these country guys had seen in a long time. They didn't dare offend me; 1) for fear I'd up and leave and 2) the occasional menacing stare from Caine might have helped. Four hours is a lot of time to spend with a bunch of strangers, but I reminded myself of the tips I'd had from Sadie. I'd smile sweetly at the guys as I approached their little groups, chat to them about trivial things for a few minutes, then leave them saying I had to pop away across the room to get their mate a beer. I rejoin them about half an hour later on my rounds.

They were intrigued by my Pommy accent, keen to know all about me and what I was doing in their beautiful country. I could hardly go telling them that I'd walked out of an unhappy marriage, that I was a police woman on a career break, that I still possessed my warrant ID card and that I'd be returning to my job in a years time. If I was to broadcast this fact then I may have no job to return to. I set about creating a new persona.

I was Michelle, the twenty-something backpacker come suit-caser from London. I'd given up my job working as a Bank Teller (cashier to you and I) in Greenwich and I'd educate them with the facts about Greenwich Mean Time. I'd tell stories about those crazy Brits who'd drink their beer warm. I'd never admit that after leaving them I was going home to bed after doing a bit of ironing. Instead I'd claim I was off to some wild party with my many equally wild friends. Photographs were inevitable, so I'd willingly pose on the basis that I wear my sunnies (sunglasses) as they'd conceal my identity to some degree, should the photos end up on the internet.

As this particular job ran into its final hour, Caine took me to one side saying,

"Now sweetie, these guys think you're great and have been asking if you do nude. It's okay, you don't have to, but it's usual at these sort of things."

I questioned Caine, asking what he thought I should do and how much I should charge. He explained that it was usual for the girl to go around with an empty jug and ask the guys for money to persuade them to get their pants off. I took a few moments to consider the proposal, taking into account that they'd already got full sight of my boobs and arse. With the tiny g-string I had on, it was just a little triangle that remained to be uncovered. I went around with the jug as coins and notes were enthusiastically thrown in. I passed the jug to Caine who quickly counted up the contents.

"You've got just over a hundred and fifty in here sweetie. You don't have to do it though. It's up to you."

One hundred and fifty dollars! That was loads extra and much more than I'd anticipated collecting. The removal of the triangle was worth that. I went into a side room and slipped off the g-string, screwing it up in my bag. My high healed shoes remained and I stood more upright than ever to ensure the really rude bits were tucked neatly away from view, then I was out there.

Of course there were many attempts from the guys to get me to bend over. They formed a large circle, tossing a coin into the centre, betting on heads or tails and getting me to pick the coin up. Perhaps disappointingly for them, I did so in the most lady like fashion, bending the knees and avoiding too much underneath exposure.

The job was a success and I left on a high. Within a couple of weeks I'd gone from a prude barmaid to a full on nudey waitress. Caine and I returned to the hotel to drop off my bag and count out the takings. He neither asked nor hinted at expecting a cut of my winnings. This had been easy money and there was lots of it. I had a huge pile of $2 coins and handed them to Caine, telling him he'd be doing me a favour by taking them from me as I didn't want to weigh down my purse. I would not take no as an answer and ordered him to accept the money as my employee for the evening. After all, he'd been my driver and many a stripper needed one of those. After a few whole hearted refusals he submitted.

So with both Caine and I fully laden with a stash of cash, we went downstairs to the bar for a well deserved drink. Two young skimpies stood serving. They didn't look anything special, if anything a bit on the scrawny side. They were friendly enough, telling us that they were backpackers from England and worked through an agency, mainly working in the more remote country pubs as the wages were better. I remained coy about my takings that evening. I worked out that I had the potential to earn a lot more cash then them by working for Sadie. As I chatted to these girls, the landlord approached me and asked if I could go the other side of the bar to work for the following hour. He offered me a good financial deal and with my new found confidence, I was flipping and raking in yet more cash. My line was,

"Heads I lose and I keep your money but flash my boobs. Tails I win and I don't flash my boobs but still keep your money . . .

Five dollars and it's a dead cert where I keep your money and you definitely see my boobs!"

That night Caine and I slept in the same room. We didn't really have any other option as it was the only room available. He remained a gentleman throughout, pulling the beds well away from one another and turning his back to give me privacy when I was getting changed or dressed, regardless of the fact he'd already seen it all some hours earlier.

Caine and I were friends for little more than a week or so. Not because we fell out of favour, but I suspect he'd been warned off by a slightly possessive Luke, who was perhaps hoping I might progress to being his girlfriend. I enjoyed the brief friendship I shared with Caine. He was the one to escort me to his recommended body piercing studio to have a nipple piecing. To say this experience resembled what I'd liken to a big red hot poker tearing through my nipple would be an understatement. However, I hoped the focus of a daring piercing would take away from that fact that my boobs were nothing special and on the small side in comparison with the other girls. I had the undersized saggy boobs, cellulite padding my arse and back of thighs, bat wing arms, hands more suited to someone twice my age and an upper lip that needed regular taming. That said, I had good skin, unlike the Aussie girls who'd leathered in the harsh sun and I looked a little younger than my years. I had a pretty face, cute blonde bob, a bit of height to me, flat stomach and my ace card was personality and substance. There were some much prettier, big chested girls out there on the circuit, but variety is the spice of life and there was a market for us all.

CHAPTER SIX

MILLENIUM

I'D BEEN IN AUSTRALIA for just two weeks. I had a job, car, mobile phone and new found friends. All that was remaining was to find some permanent accommodation. I was initially staying with my parents' friends, a couple nearing their sixties whom I had little in common with. I was keen to be around people more my own age and Luke offered a solution.

"There's a room going at my place. One of the guys has just been sent to jail, so won't be returning for a while."

This was a house share for four in Joondalup, situated in a great position, less than half an hour from the city centre and about ten minutes drive from Tommy's place. The rent was cheap, very cheap, but the room was grubby and in need of a good clean out. I completed an economy mini makeover on my 8' x 10' allocated space and bought myself a basic CD player and room fan. I was given a shelf in the fridge and half a layer of the freezer. I shared cutlery with cockroaches and declined to make use of the outdoor pool, unsure what lurked in those murky waters. I now felt happy, bordering on content, for I had everything I needed. Having few possessions meant little responsibility, commitment or concern.

Fitness remained of importance to me, more so than ever now that my body was the tool of my trade. Joondalup had a large leisure centre with an outdoor running track. Routine set in, starting my mornings with ten laps of the track, followed by my floor work consisting of numerous press ups and sit ups. The occasional meeting with a pre-historic looking creature was inevitable, with a morning greeting from a stumpy tailed lizard or slightly smaller yet equally dragon like reptile hissing at me.

My little police diary became full of scribbled bookings and I found myself working with other girls. My first job with Cindy was in the forest area of Perth. Cindy was a pretty girl with a casual blonde bob and cheeky little smile. We were both booked for two hours topless, but she talked the guys into passing around the jug for us to spend the last half an hour nude. Cindy had a little giggle as I stood with her totally starkers, suggesting my neatly trimmed triangle was very European and advised that expectations were for girls to go Brazilian or her preference, Hollywood.

So, by the next job my nether regions had gone all American and a new turmoil was upon me, which was shared by many of the girls. Hot weather and frequent shaving equalled in-growers and evil shaving rash. It became routine to make up my face and the lower half, with a dab of foundation here and a bit of tinted powder there.

I was picking up tips all the time. I'd never leave money unattended in my bag, but keep it with me. I made a little zip-up sparkly wrist cuff where I'd stash the cash if it was too hot to wear boots, which were the preferred more practical option. My car key would remain with me at all times as I never knew if I'd have to leave in a hurry, naked or not. At least I could do a runner to my car to get away.

I'd suss out the Mr Nice Guy in the crowd. He would be the one I'd turn to if there was a problem. I'd be prompt, both in my arrival and departure, but avoid looking at my watch so as to appear care free and enjoying being there. However, I would candidly glance at the guys wrists, keeping check so as to be out of there as soon as the clock struck time.

Any drinks I had would be discarded once left for a moment unattended. Perhaps I'd select something alcoholic, tip most away, then pretend to sip on it. This gave the appearance that I was in the party sprit and I'd even act a little tipsy to keep up the pretence.

Everything was going brilliantly, securing a job, car, housing and friends in a matter of weeks. It felt quite an achievement, except there was one niggling problem and it wasn't going to leave me anytime soon. There was a phone line at my Joondalup home and I was just a call away from the other side of the world. The daily calls would persist and the ever emotional pressure was coming from all directions, being told,

"You should be back home sorting out your marriage."

"The shame of it, you getting your ginny out and showing everyone, how degrading."

"Darling, I love and adore you and I'm so sorry for all the hurt I've caused. I want to support you with your pursuits, but I miss you so much."

"I'll be waiting patiently by the phone for you to call me tomorrow."

I was completely honest about my new job with Neil and my family, not because I was attempting to provoke a hostile response or annoy them, but because I was so proud of my achievements; that I had the guts to do such a job and that people actually thought I was attractive enough to pay for my company. Neil responded positively, sounding supportive and understanding, yet my father did not share this attitude, which on reflection is understandable. I expect most fathers would have shared his displeasure. I was determined that I was not going to be bullied into a premature departure and assured my family that Neil and I would be fine, that he could come and visit me in Australia in a few months and that I simply needed this time to get my head around things before I returned to the marital home. I found this response appeased all and allowed me to have some respite from their brainwashing attempts.

With Christmas and the new Millennium almost upon us, the many party invites were keeping me pre-occupied and served as a spirit uplifter. I spent Christmas Day with Luke and his family and after dinner we sunbathed out by the pool in the blazing heat. This day and the forthcoming week served as some welcomed rest and relaxation, which I hadn't actually had since my arrival in the country. Tommy had a pool party at his place on the Boxing Day and by New Years Eve I was off to a fancy dress party, with the theme of film characters. My new friend Frank arrived to collect me, dressed as a Viking without the all important hat and asking for my help. Moments later, the kitchen cupboards were raided for the colander, tin foil and tape and in no time horns were attached and the costume was complete.

I already had animal print fur from my earlier ears and tail creations, so made a short jagged hemmed skirt, with a little pocket at the front to store my cigarettes and toy Cheater. I covered a bra in the fur and wore a long hair piece, matted slightly to give that authentic just 'come from the jungle' look. I became Jane, hoping that I might meet a loin clothed Tarzan.

There was momentary horror as I arrived to find what appeared to be another Jane. It seemed the animal print material was very popular that night. With speedy introductions I was relieved to be meeting Wilma, with her husband Fred Flintstone by her side. Austin Powers was entertaining the guests on the Karaoke and James Bond was topping up the glasses.

It was a rather mysterious d'Artagnan that caught my eye, with his long flowing locks. He wore a feathered cap, white ruffled shirt, with the cuffs hanging partially over his hands, heavy cape and spurs attached to his long boots. From time to time he'd remove the cap and wig to show off neatly cropped brown hair, with a few gelled flecks of sun bleached blonde at the front. A Kurt Russell dimple on his chin was covered with two day growth of stubble and occasionally his eyes would go into an uncontrollable blinking fit, exposing a vulnerability that I warmed to. He sipped on his drink, a Jim Beam and Coke, whilst I had whatever was going. About an hour into the evening we finally met.

"Hi, I'm Jane and my Tarzan has failed to show up this evening. I might just need protecting by a Musketeer. Would you know any?" I enquired.

"Hi, I'm Daniel, pleased to meet you. It's Michelle isn't it? They've been talking about you in these circles." he replied.

To which I responded, *"All good things I hope, like that I'm actually a very famous celebrity in the UK and achiever of great things."*

Daniel claimed he was six feet tall, yet even with his heeled boots he was just a couple of inches taller than me. His baggy clothing gave him some much needed bulk as on closer inspection he was actually very slim. He spoke in what I can only describe as a posh Aussie accent; if there is such a thing. He had this knack of speaking in a quiet, gentle tone, so I could just about hear him if I stood really close. He later told me he did that deliberately. Friends called him Daniel and

I rightly assumed he was not a fan of any abbreviations, so avoided the temptation of calling him Dan or Danny.

His strong spatula shaped hands suggested his employment involved something manual. He explained he was a panel beater, restoring luxury and vintage cars and was regarded as one of the best in the business. He spoke of a public school education, outside business interests in tea-tree oil, with a few other business ideas in fruition. He boasted that he owned a 1950's sports car which he kept at his riverside home in a desirable suburb of Perth.

As the party got into full swing a live band was entertaining us with Rhythm and Blues, that's when I saw Daniel's hand slip into his right trouser pocket and pull out a little harmonica. He began playing in time with the band across the other side of the room. Daniel passed me his number, inviting me to see him perform with his own band at a pub in central Perth, telling me that he knew influential people in the music business. I popped the number into my front pocket next to Cheater and with the eruption of fireworks it was midnight and a new Millennium had began.

CHAPTER SEVEN

I BELIEVE THAT FATE HAS
BROUGHT US HERE

FOR A COUPLE OF days after the party, I found myself thinking about Daniel. Not for any love struck reason, but because I thought he sounded like a good catch. Someone who would be worth knowing and could perhaps introduce me to some of those influential people he'd been telling me about. I gave him a call and was rather disappointed when the answer phone kicked. I'd failed to rehearse what I was going to say and feared some ridiculous blurb was about to come out of my mouth. I considered putting the phone down, but it was too late, the answer phone was already recording my momentary silence, so I went for it.

"Hi Daniel, not sure if you remember me, but I'm Jane from the party . . . It's Michelle actually, but there you go. Your gig at The Central in Perth, I'm up for going. Give me a call to let me know the details."

Daniel called me back later that same day, sounding more affluent than I'd remembered. I've always been a bit of a sucker for voices and accents, which started in my cadet years when I had a crush on the first aid instructor for his Somerset accent. I met with Daniel a few days later, turning up at The Central to watch him perform. There were just a handful of people in the audience and the band consisted of an odd mix of characters. With a bongo drummer, guitarist, lead singer and Daniel. Sensing disappointment from the poor turn out, I tried to encourage enthusiasm among the few spectators, frantically clapping and cheering in all the right places with a bit of animated foot tapping when I got into the beat. As I watched and listened, I noticed just how erotic the harmonica actually is. Lips pursed around the tiny instrument, blowing, sucking and using the tongue to create the harmonious vibrations on this organ. Mmmmm, back to reality!

We saw one another almost every day after that. Daniel had some time off work over the holiday season and I had no more bookings, none whatsoever. I had my savings to keep me going, but just needed to be frugal for now. The young Luke and I had been dining out at Burger King and Uncle Sam's. However, I was now being taken out for some fine dining at restaurants in the prosperous parts of town and Daniel was always insistent on picking up the bill. He'd take me to meet his friends and it was refreshing to finally be around people my own age.

Daniel was aware of my circumstances and I'd frequently discuss my dilemma with him and friends. My family had always taken a sympathetic attitude towards Neil for his betrayal towards me, yet I was now hearing some conflicting views and advice.

"He sounds like a dick head. Why would you want to go back to someone like him? He'll only do it again and again."

"Any guy who does that to a woman has a complete lack of respect for them."

"No matter how hard you try, you'll never be able to totally trust him again."

"Once a liar, always a liar. A leopard never changes his spots."

Deep down, I knew Neil and I were over, yet I didn't know how my family would ever allow me to be free from him. Anytime I made attempts to end it, they'd protest how hurt they were and my refusals to totally forgive Neil were causing *them* so much anguish.

After a handful of diner dates, Daniel invited me for a trip to the beautiful Margaret River wine region, which I excitedly accepted. He booked a fabulous hotel room, which came with room spa, fluffy dressing gowns and luxury bathroom products as standard.

The drive down to Margaret River was about four hours away. Yet again we were getting around in my old banger, whilst his sports car remained in the garage and the other on his driveway.

It was only half way into the return trip that Daniel finally offered to take over at the wheel.

"I have to be a bit careful though," he warned,

"just in case the cops are about . . . because I'm not supposed to drive at the moment, I'm disqualified."

First off, I assumed disqualification was due to a drink driving offence or perhaps he'd been caught driving his sports car like a maniac. However, I learnt that his failure to pay speeding fines had resulted in an automatic disqualification.

This slight tarnish of his character wasn't going to put me off, in fact I warmed to this bad boy image and was growing to enjoy his company. We'd sit out on his veranda, sipping wine and watching the sunset reflect against the river, chatting for hours about our hopes and aspirations. His home felt like a safe house; there was no unwanted barrage of calls from the UK and no one telling me to restore my marriage with Neil.

Neil had been threatening to get a spur of the moment flight to Perth and he knew my Joondalup address, but I was safe at Daniel's. They didn't know about him. So, I began spending more and more time at Daniel's. I'd go back to his home after a meal, with all good intentions of driving back to my lodgings in Joondalup, but then he'd ply me with wine and I'd have no choice but to stay. After several weeks of dodging the UK calls and spending so little time away from Daniel, I decided I had to be strong and stand up to the bullies. My hands shook and tears rolled down my cheeks as I made the call . . .

I see little point in going through what the dialogue may or may not have been, because it is something of a blur in my memory. There were a lot of tears, pleading yet again for forgiveness and that I was obviously confused and didn't really want out of the marriage, but the words from my mouth which changed everything, which finally got me heard and taken seriously and sounded louder and clearer than anything else I'd previously said were,

"I've met someone else."

That was it. That made it final and Neil was now willing to let me go. I doubt he wanted me anymore with the knowledge that someone else had my affections. Of course the calls didn't stop, but instead it was from my father, wanting to known the details, belittling Daniel, the person he knew nothing about and discrediting me for going off with someone else and not being at home to sort things out. I became a huge disappointment and had apparently brought *dishonour* on the family. I could deal with that rejection. After all, I'd become rather hardened to it, having been a rejected wife for years without actually knowing it at the time. I got emotional mail from my dad, begging and pleading that I would return home if I truly loved my family. I refused to allow my dad to dictate what I should or should not do and with Daniel's continued support I remained strong to this resolve.

Within a matter of weeks, Neil announced that he too had met someone else; a pretty girl twelve years his junior. With her appearance in the equation came a more supportive attitude from my dad, who seemed to have discarded his Team Neil shirt and would occasionally wear Team Michelle.

As time went on, the emotionally charged calls became less frequent, a solicitor got involved and the house went up for sale, selling relatively quickly. I was not in a position to particularly have my pick of possessions, so had to hope that some personal effects would be kept for me, having to accept that I'd be more likely to get the rotten end of the deal. The final insult being that in divorce proceedings, I was recorded as being the unfaithful one, because I had abandoned my husband for Daniel and Neil retained the title of The Innocent Party.

I felt indebted to Daniel, for providing the safe house, the emotional support, the distraction and being the *someone else* in my life. I think for those reasons, I excused our incompatibility. You know when a couple look good together side by side? Well we didn't.

I like to be relatively structured and organised in life and routine, even down to the way my tea towels are folded and the fact I even iron bath towels, underwear and socks. However, Daniel's life and organisational skills were in a state of chaos and I didn't like that. He had a stack of unopened letters under his bed and when I finally persuaded him to pull his head out of the sand and open them, they exposed a mountain of payment requests and unpaid bills. They'd even progressed to final demands and bailiff letters. His head fell into his hands in despair, saying that he could see no way out of all his problems. He explained that he went to work, worked hard for many hours of the day and found he had no hours left to get around to paying bills, which then increased with the default charges. He said that the only way he could cope was to ignore all of that and just carry on working.

It was hard to establish how he'd accrued so much debt. He didn't have nice clothes, in fact, I'd noticed most were in disrepair after I'd pulled the crumpled mass out of his wardrobe to iron and fold them neatly back, stitching holes where needed. His sports car in the garage was a 1960's

Chevrolet Camaro, that had huge rust patches and had become his slow moving restoration project. The other car on his driveway was nothing special, more of a mothers shopping car. He spoke of no exotic holidays, nor possessed the latest boys toys. He lived in a nice home, but until recently had two lodgers covering two thirds of the rent, so the extravagant rental property wouldn't have caused his downfall. It seemed his inability to organise his life had created the money worries he now faced.

I had the power to wave a magic wand and resolve the financial problems, which I did. I have had previous experience for doing this sort of thing and I question what I have gained from such generosity. I can only assume it's a type of obsessive trait I display, the same as my need to iron tea towels and socks, to seek order and fulfil a need to take control. I paid off the debts, but it didn't seem to make everything better. Daniel's problems were more deep seated.

I told Daniel of my plans to move on and reminded him that I would eventually be returning to the UK at the end of my career break. With that, he appeared more vulnerable than ever, with eyes blinking uncontrollably and a smell of fear emanating from him. Daniel said he would drop everything and come with me, that he couldn't face me leaving, unable to cope with rejection for a second time in his life.

He went into detail about an ex-girlfriend who had abandoned their relationship and fled to Europe, never to be seen again and that a very dark period in his life had followed. He spoke about death and just how close he'd come to quite literally taking a leap to end it all.

Around the time of the affairs revelation, when emotions were heightened, Neil had spoken about killing himself if he couldn't be with me. I am in no doubt that there was no substance in Neil's threats and this was just something said from the anguish at that time. However, when Daniel spoke of suicide, there was a fearful look in his eyes of loneliness and despair. I got a distinct feeling that there were indeed times in his life when he was a frightened soul, having nowhere else to go and needing to be rid of the torment of his inner turmoil forever.

I knew that feeling of rejection to some degree. Neil discarded me for one of his many mistresses throughout our marriage. I felt abandoned by my disloyal dad who had made my choice to leave Neil a very difficult one. I knew what it was to feel emotional hurt and pain and I couldn't bare to see Daniel in such distress.

I was faced with a dilemma, to follow my head and remind myself that Daniel's problems were not mine. That I hadn't known him long enough to devote my energies to such a needy person. If he was to choose to kill himself, then I'd probably never get to hear about it in any case.

I chose to follow my heart. I thought that I had perhaps been sent as his Saviour. He had no family in Perth and many of his friends had become intolerant of his unreliability and were having less to do with him. I would have blamed myself if my departure had led to a tragic ending for Daniel.

I went with him to see his doctor who diagnosed him with clinical depression. Daniel was given medication, which he'd often forget to take, complaining that the tablets were the cause of his terrible night sweats. His appetite was poor and he sustained himself with milk and jelly sweets. When I managed to persuade him to eat home cooked food, he would be left with the discomfort of indigestion.

I tried and tried to keep Daniel motivated. He kept saying that he wanted to come to the UK with me and agreeing to this gave him a goal and a positive outlook. The simplest solution to allow Daniel to live and work in the UK was for us to be married. By now I'd taken a rather low regard to marriage law, feeling that so many people broke the rules and that it was simply a piece of paper. I was quite happy to accept this proposal and towards the end of my stay, Daniel and I went to Perth Registry Office to get married, with Tommy as witness.

Daniel was so preoccupied with his work that it was only on the Big Day that he went out to buy a tie. I bought my own ring, selecting one from the five dollar bargain bin. It was decorated with a big blue flower and coated in plastic. After the short ceremony and celebration lunch, still dressed in my white lace frock, I left the venue. I had a busy afternoon and evening work schedule, which was going to pay for the days events. Daniel had promised that he'd arrange a proper wedding ceremony during our Thailand honeymoon, so I packed a decent dress and purchased the gold bands. But just like most things Daniel was supposed to do, it never happened.

Once the wedding paperwork was complete, Daniel's UK Visa could be processed before my time was up. He kept his promise to give up work as we were supposed to travel around the country during my final months. But once again, this never went as arranged. Instead, Daniel became focused on plans to start a metal work business in the UK and now devoted his energies, enthusiasm and much of my finances to preparing for this project, by building and purchasing machinery ready for shipment.

At times I struggled to conceal my disappointment about the failings in our relationship. I was gutted about the cancelled road trip, and even suggesting that I should return to the UK without him and us go our separate ways. Of course this would follow with Daniel collapsing into an emotional heap, me feeling sorry for him and him promising that we would eventually travel. He'd suggest our time in the UK would be spent earning enough money so we could return to Oz to do all the travelling we wanted and live happily ever after.

As the new Mrs Daniel, I went to visit the in-laws, who lived in a remote town on the other side of the country. Daniel was keen to impress and show me off as some sort of trophy, so on his advice, I wore the little black dress, high heeled shoes and designer handbag for my début appearance as his wife. It didn't take me long to realise this was an inappropriate outfit and probably gave out the wrong first impression to this insular community of people, who were likely to stereotype me as some sort of brainless bimbo.

A welcome home party had been arranged and a group of family and friends had gathered in the garden of his parents home. I was ushered to a patio table and chairs by the kitchen door, where the women and children were seated. Daniel and the other men wandered off into the shed and were waited on by female guests who were taking over the occasional tray of hot sausage rolls and snacks. As the sun set, the children disappeared to bed and a small group of women remained, swigging on their cans of Moonshine and taking on feral characteristics. There appeared to be an urge for them to act like domineering blokes. Maybe so as to serve some need for power and importance. Had they forgotten that they'd spent the day running around after their fellas with the trays of food?

Some were untamed, ungroomed, foulmouthed, with a brash accent and a cackle for laughter. They wore baggy shirts and for the ones that did bother to wear a bra, it was sure to be an ill fitting one. They could of course drink any man under the table. This was not the image of all those women, but certainly paints the picture of those who were keeping me entertained by their insular archaic attitudes. One of those women was a manager for one of the pubs in town and was explaining that from time to time she had to hire in Skimpy bairmaids,

"I don't like Skimpies", she croaked.

I attempted to reassure her, *"Skimpies are just providing the service that you order. Someone's got to do it and from what I've seen, there are a lot of nice intelligent girls in that business . . . and I'm not a bad person."*

"Yeah, but I still don't like Skimpies."

Although most of the women were pleasant and welcoming enough, they were not overly engaging in conversation with me. Not for wanting to be aloof, but because they struggled to understand my accent (I didn't even think I had one!). I saw little to be gained in trying to reason with this ice maiden and her fixed attitudes; I didn't see the point in wasting my breath as it made no difference to me that I didn't meet her approval.

With the sounds of unknown creatures squawking and clicking in the darkness under the stars, the numbers diminished. Daniel and the remaining men had crawled out of the shed and were now seated around a camp fire. One of them was strumming on a guitar and Daniel was fiddling with his harmonica, occasionally putting it to his lips to draw and blow the random note here and there. The mood was mellow and I was loving it.

"Isn't it about time you ran along now and left us men to it?" mumbled John, Daniel's younger brother, who appeared to command undeserved respect from his family.

"I'm quite happy to stay out here for a bit thanks," I said in a polite but firm tone.

"No, I don't think you get it. You're not welcome out here anymore. Us men want some time together without you being around," demanded John.

Daniel could no longer pretend not to hear this conversation as the volume turned up a notch or four.

"You might want to talk to me in some sexist way, like I'm some little woman. But it's not something I'm accustomed to and would like to be spoken to with some respect," I said in retaliation.

Daniel just stood there, pathetically, failing to fight my corner and stand up to his rude brother. Moments earlier

I'd felt chilled and relaxed, but was now forced to scuttle off like a naughty girl being sent to my room. Although John's confrontation became common knowledge in the family, I never got an apology. It was simply something not to be discussed further, giving the unsaid word that John's behaviour that night had been acceptable.

Daniel's father would say very little to me. Not that he really had much to say to anyone, spending his days tinkering around in his shed, working on his collection of vintage cars. It was the mother who seemed to hold the family together, earning the money, looking after the grandchildren and doing the household chores. The family would chat superficially to me, but not in any depth or great interest and didn't appear to value my thoughts and opinions. For them it was all about their son Daniel, what I could offer and how I should look after him. I could tell the mother worried about Daniel, not because he was with me and I think that was something of a relief to her. I got the impression that as the sensitive soul in the family, she saw Daniel as the vulnerable one. I assured her that I would look after him as best I could. I meant those words at the time and I think that was a comfort to her.

We had some fun during our visit. This remote inland town was situated on a river and we'd go kayaking, swing from the ropes in the over hanging trees and swim in its brown waters. We'd admire the many cruising house boats and even went sunbathing on one for the day. These boats were like floating cubes, complete with lounge, bedroom, bathroom and sundeck. We went on a short road trip to visit The Rellies and that's when I was taken to the most unimaginable outback settlements, with their unmade dusty roads and rickety timber houses balancing on stilts. We travelled through towns that looked as if they'd been preserved for over a hundred years from the Gold Rush era.

Before the end of the stay we travelled to the awe inspiring Kings Canyon with its brilliant orange rock formations looking like some ancient oriental ruins. Once I'd set eyes on Uluru at sunrise, I felt content that I'd seen all that I needed to of this fantastic country for now, until the next visit.

Chapter Eight

HIGHER THAN I'VE BEEN
BEFORE

"*Would you like to see my menu for today?*" I asked, standing tall and confidently, resting one hand casually against the beer pump.

"*I can offer the two dollar flip, but you may lose your money and see absolutely nothing,*" I purred with an animated disappointed frown.

"*There are of course the five dollar specials where there is no disappointment at all. For five dollars you can watch me play ice cube Scalextrics or Cheeky Cheezels. The choice is yours.*"

I could hear the rustle and clink of coins and notes,
"*Or I have the two dollar slot machine.*"

I pulled on the elastic at the front of my knickers and indicated that the coins need to be aimed into my underwear. I stood a safe distance of about six feet away, with the bar between me and the eager customers, as those tiny coins got tossed in. That was $10 and I'd only just started.

"*I'll go for the ice cube thing,*" said the white haired chubby guy perched on the bar stool. Offering up a beer dampened note, I snatched it up and tucked it into the top of my boot. I pulled the largest ice cube I could find out of the bucket and said,

"*Okay, this is the car I've chosen for our Scalextrics ride.*"

The drill began as I pulled down my bra, exposing my boobs and began rubbing the ice cube around my left nipple,

"*The car is going round and round the roundabout . . .*"
I moved the ice cube over to the right nipple,

"*It's done a stunt jump over the valley . . . and round and round another roundabout.*"

I pushed my elbows into my sides to squeeze my boobs together and slid the dripping cube into my cleavage.

"*We're driving into the dark valley . . . Oh, the car has crashed!*"

I quickly pulled my bra up, announcing "*Show's over.*"

Another pinky was placed on the bar.

"*I'll go for the cheeky Cheezle,*" said the guy in the faded blue vest top and mullet hair.

I came prepared with my props and opened a fresh bag of the cheese flavoured corn snacks, which were a bit like gigantic Hullahoops. The bra got pulled down again and I placed a Cheezle on each nipple. With a cheeky grin, looking the customer in the eye, I clasped one hand underneath my breast, pulled it upwards, then tilted my head to the side and snatched up the cheesy snack with my mouth on one side, then the other. Easy money. That was $30 in the first five minutes in addition to the wages I was already due. Now, some reading this may be horrified at this immoral behaviour by the former Christian Mormon girl. But before you condemn me, please take into consideration that this was good money and any regular job for a backpacker would have pay so little in comparison. I would have considered it a travesty if I'd spent my career break spending my days fruit picking on a remote farm for a pittance of a wage.

After the busy Christmas period, the toppo and skimpy work dried up. I got a couple of hours of pub work here and there, but never really knew until a few days earlier whether I was going to be earning anything for the week. Sadie said this was the usual trend for that time of the year. Even the experienced strippers like herself had to go further afield for work. She had just got back from a five day trip to Kalgoolie. This was a mining town about two hours flight away. She explained that she'd go there with another girl, skimpy behind the bars, then pick up stripping jobs from the guys in the evening. She wasn't keen on being away from home, so made sure they worked as hard as possible to clean up. She wasn't talking domestic chores here; the miners earned a good wage. After a long hard shift there was nothing more in the remote settlement to entertain them except for beer and girls, who came at a price. The miners had the money, so the girls scammed as much as they could from them.

I was new to this trade, not an experienced stripper like Sadie. The Kalgoolie run was not an option for me. Sadie introduced me to a skimpy agency, the same one that those scrawny backpackers in Collie had worked through. I got a few jobs from that agency, but had to keep myself available exclusively to them for my work. Their rates of pay were poor in comparison, with a big chunk of commission taken from me. So I pulled out after a few weeks, as I found myself forced to turn down better paid jobs I was being offered through the other girls.

As I worked in a few more pubs, I built up contacts and would be phoned directly to do bar work. I built up a reputation for being prompt and reliable and most importantly, a good worker. I got respect from the regular bar staff as I worked as hard as them. I'd be serving the customers, filling the dishwasher, lifting the glass filled crates to the fridge and emptying the ash-trays. In between this hard graft, I'd whop my boobs out, make suggestive, flirtatious, tongue in cheek comments and generally keep the customers well entertained. I'd get the occasional lecture of, 'how could I stoop so low to flaunt my body?' from a disgruntled low paid regular bar tender. But I was over all of that. It was up to me what I did and I was simply providing a service that was required.

One day in February, I got a two hour job at a back street bar in a less than affluent suburb. I entered the dingy looking locals pub, initially being hit by the smell of stale tobacco and booze. This was not unusual to many of the pubs I'd worked in and I smiled confidently at the small gathering of scruffy men in their fifties and sixties, seated beside the sterile looking stainless steel bar. As per usual, I made my way into the ladies toilets and shut myself into a cramped cubicle to change into my showgirl underwear. I had a bag full of different outfits and would chose the most appropriate bra and knickers set to suit the clientele.

I chose the cream lace set with the pink bow in the centre of the cleavage. I checked my watch and had a few minutes to spare, so looked in the mirror to check that my long blonde hair piece was in place, recoated my red lips, reached into my bra cups to perk up my boobs and sprayed some cheap sweet smelling perfume around my fake tanned body. A little bit of glitter mist twinkled on my shoulders and just above my bra. I was looking good. However, for the first time in ages I could feel the evil unwanted adrenaline rising up my body and into my arms. My heart began pounding and hands trembling. Shit! What could I do? I tried calm thoughts.

There was nothing intimidating about this venue nor the old chaps lined up eagerly awaiting my stint at their bar, so what the hell was the problem with me? I had to work through this. With a faked confidence, I trotted out behind the bar and was given a run down of the prices and how the till worked.

With my first drinks order I clasped the beer glass more firmly than ever and pulled the pump down. I put all my concentration into trying to keep my hand as steady as possible, but as soon as I moved the glass away from the pump and onto the bar top, my hands trembled and the bar towel soaked up some of the inevitable spillage that followed. The involuntary hand shaking was filling my thoughts and frustrations, but I powered through it. I completed my shift, but was never invited back to that pub again.

I was so annoyed with myself. The anxiety attacks were back with me at a time I really could do without them. I went to a natural therapy shop and was recommended a liquid to drink, which was expensive, yet ineffective. I thought back to my beginnings in this trade and remembered the alco-pop remedy for nerves. I went to the bottle shop and purchased a small bottle of vodka, which now formed part of my kit bag. Whenever I felt the anxiety creeping in before a job, I'd take a couple of gulps of neat vodka straight from the bottle, then suck on an extra strong mint to take away any alcohol breath. I found this to do the trick and would not go anywhere without this comforter of a magic potion, just in case I needed it. I'd usually be going to work on an empty stomach, so as not to have a bloated tummy. Therefore, the couple of mouthfuls would go straight to my head, yet I would remain safely below the drink drive limit. Breath testing road blocks on the major routes were common place during the evenings and I could not afford to lose my licence.

I'd hand out Sadie's business cards at the pubs and in turn I'd get calls for toppo work at the customers homes when they were having a blokes get together, Bucks Night (Stag night to you and I), or maybe a boat cruise out to Rottness Island or the Swan River. I would only ever do the boat trips on Sadie's recommendation, as she knew the clients from old. I felt reassured that I was safe to be captive on their boat if Sadie had vetted them first. The boat trips were good because they'd generally be in the day time with a booking for at least six hours. I would get an all over sun tan and still be available for the more common evening work. The down side was that I would be left with a swaying feeling for the entire day, having stood for hours on end, being rocked from side to side by the waves.

I worked with some gorgeous girls. Stella was about five feet tall, with blonde wavy hair that reached past her bum. She was Sadie's stripper friend, and when she wasn't doing a duo act with Sadie, she'd have a strip routine that consisted of some mind boggling bendy moves. She had the ability to do the splits, then flip her legs around her neck. By day she was a busy mum with two kids, yet by night she'd go out stripping and her husband would be her driver.

Carla was a tall Romanian-Australian girl with a slight Eastern European accent and long brunette hair. Although she didn't have the most impressive boobs, her long slender legs went to the tops of her armpits. She was friends with Tammy, who was a mixed race Asian-Australian. Tammy had a beautiful figure enhanced by her coffee skin tone and was untouched by a surgeons knife. She'd call me with the occasional pub job.

One of the most intriguing characters was Melody. She was the oldest of the girls, being in her mid-thirties. She was a single mum and would sometimes bump into clients at jobs who she'd recognise from her school run. Melody's self confessed role model was Pamela Anderson, yet she was the more attractive version. She was petite and short, with long blonde cotton wool textured hair. She had the tiniest of waists and I suspect she may have had a couple of ribs removed to achieve this. She had pert D cup boobs with perfectly positioned protruding nipples. Her skin was pale and smooth, make-up immaculate with the use of indulgent products from her beautician. She would portray a vulnerable girly character to the clients who in turn would want to be generous and protective towards her.

She would be sure to do a deal on her arrival, ensuring she got a guaranteed nude second hour, by pricing herself a little below the usual fee. Just before she was due to remove her g-string, she would chat to the guys and give a selected few a sneak preview of the inside of her knickers, so they felt extra special by this advanced treat.

Of all the girls, it was Sadie who I admired and trusted the most. It was usual for me to be at a toppo job and for Sadie to turn up as the booked stripper, accompanied by her thuggish looking driver. She would look like she'd just stepped out from a trendy nightclub, dressed in tight shiny black trousers, fitted red jacket, flowing blonde hair and a cute white smile. She'd be shown into a private room where she'd be introduced to the Stag or Birthday Boy. She'd run through some important instructions with him,

"Now, during my routine, I'll be sitting on your lap and will be guiding you where to place your hands and when to remove them," explained Sadie to the guy.

"There will be no other grabbing and touching otherwise the show is over. When I get to the fruit and veg part of the show, you'll get to eat the banana. If you attempt to put your mouth anywhere else, then again, show over," she warned in her friendly, yet matter of fact tone.

"It's gonna be fun and you'll have a great time as long as you stick to the rules."

112

The guys would eagerly form a semi-circle and the boom box would begin pumping out the dance music to mark the start of the routine.

The sound of Sonique floods the room,

"You always make me smile, when I'm feeling down, you give me such a vibe . . . Your love it feels so good . . . and that's what takes me high!"

Sadie would come dancing in with her PVC Fantasy Cop outfit, four inch platform shiny stiletto shoes and cartwheel into the centre of the spectators. An intro into the chorus of the song marked the next part of the routine, with a piece of clothing removed at the given times. A chair would be placed into the centre stage and she'd take the hand of the selected guy, who would be instructed to be seated. Sadie would sit on his lap, clothed in just her stockings, bra and g-string and take hold of his hands and place them on top her bra. Still keeping a firm grip of his hands, she would pull the bra off, revealing her big bouncy boobs. She'd dance around a bit more and do a few more cartwheels. She'd then sit on the chair, spread her legs apart and begin pulling a long string of beads from her fanny.

Whilst all this was going on, I'd stand to the back of the crowd, checking that all were kept topped up with their beers. I'd know what part of the routine Sadie was at by what song was playing. The guys became less interested in their beer as the show moved into the final stages. Sadie would be laid out on the floor, heels still on and her slender legs up in the air in a 'V' shape. The gold plated vibrator had been replaced with a carrot, then a banana. She'd reach between her legs to peel open the ripe fruit, then on cue, the selected guy knelt down and took a bite of the banana, just as her legs closed tightly around his neck to prevent his head going down any further. She'd flip herself up and this guy would become her play thing. Her hands would be tugging on the waistband of his trousers, to make just enough room at the front for her to squirt the spray cream she'd earlier had on her boobs down his trousers. She'd reach down his and tug at the top of his underpants, yanking them up as high as she could. This would all be to the amusement of the others watching. The end of the show would be marked with her placing one of her business cards between her boobs and getting the guy to remove it with his teeth. The music would end and Sadie's driver would scoop up her discarded clothing. Within half hour of her arrival she'd be off to her next job.

Although she'd play the ditsy bimbo to the clients, Sadie was one of the most astute business women I have ever met. She used to have a sensible office job. But her long term partner Cole, had encouraged and supported her into the stripping business. He'd given her the confidence that she had what it took to do such a job. She'd started off as a raunchy dancer and progressed to running her own business in this glamour industry. There was never any sex or prostitution involved in the business that she ran. There were no comparisons between her business and a brothel. Strippers and toppo waitresses cost more than prostitutes and the guys could be entertained by us without returning to their wives and girlfriends feeling guilty. During my time in this trade, there were times when I'd be offered an indecent proposal, referred to by clients as a 'bit of slap and tickle' in exchange for a large sum of cash. However, no amount of money was going to tempt me and would only serve to devalue my worth in the long term.

Around six months into my stay in Oz, I had a substantial amount of money in my bank account, with my share of the equity from the house sale in the UK and a jointly owned endowment cashed in. I decided the time had come for me to treat myself to something that was going to be all mine and no one would ever be able to take half from me at a later stage. A set of boobs was to be my prize purchase! Most of the other girls had them and offered me advice as to the recommended surgeon and size.

I flicked through porn magazines to check out boobs and help me make my choice. Within a week of my initial consultation I was in the operating theatre having the job done. By the afternoon of the op I was bandaged up and on my way home. I had a couple of half litre bottles dangling by my sides where drains had been placed under my armpits.

The first three days were the most uncomfortable. I was unable to sleep laying down, so had to be perched up by a mountain of pillows. Anything that involved pushing, pulling or reaching up was a strain, even down to the opening of a fridge or cupboard door. However, the pain was worth it and within two weeks I was back at work, confidently flashing off my lovely big new boobs. The spaniel ears B/C cups had become big bouncy E-F cups with their 400 cubic centimetre saline implant fillers.

The down side to the op was having to stay off strenuous exercise for six weeks. With limited exercise and a healthy appetite came a weight gain of about an extra ten pounds.

This was far too much to maintain in this business. Stella offered me a few of her prescription appetite suppressants, which did work for the short term, but I'd heard that this sort of amphetamine based medication could become addictive and didn't want any of that. I wasn't keen on getting back into jogging as I didn't want to ruin the new boobs, so signed up to BC Body Club. This was a well equipped gym complete with pool and spa. Keen to get my monies worth out of my monthly subscription, I went to the gym most mornings, following a work out tailor made by an instructor. Within a few weeks I was seeing notable results and getting praise from many of my regular clients.

My little diary became crammed with bookings and I'd go from one job to another, giving myself just enough time to drive to the next location. I would rarely get a day free between Wednesday to Saturday, but could usually guarantee Sunday's off. I loved those Sunday's. Daniel and I would arrange to meet friends at a beautiful location for a late buffet breakfast. We'd go to places such as The Blue Duck or Indian Tea House in Cottesloe, Co-Co's in South Perth or Frasers at Kings Park. We'd travel into Freo and have a wander around the market after our morning feast. If it had been a late finish on the Saturday night, we'd skip breakfast and make our way to a winery in the Swan Valley. We'd share a bottle and nibble on a share platter of a cheese board, cold meats and pate. Another favourite was The Jetty at Hillary's where we'd go for the all you can eat evening buffet for $25 a head.

Sometimes I went to jobs where no stripper was booked, but the guys wanted a show. If I felt safe around the clients, then I'd occasionally offer a mini show, but only if the price was right. Sometimes I'd cut a deal of getting more money and working less hours. This came as a blessing if I was working in the country and had a long drive back home.

I'd start my show already nude. With the baby lotion in my right hand, I'd begin shaking the bottle in a wanking type hand movement. I'd pour the contents gently and seductively over my breasts, moving down to my belly button to form a heart shape with the lotion. I'd place my hands onto my boobs and gently squeeze them together, before sliding my hands around my chest and torso, stopping to caress each nipple, very, very slowly. I'd glide my hands down my glistening tanned flesh, reaching in between my legs. I'd fumble for the tiny protruding pearl and begin pulling out another and another from this string of beads I'd fed into my fanny in the toilets ten minutes earlier. I'd wrap the beads around my neck so that they would dangle around my boobs. From my tool bag, I'd pull out the shiny, highly polished gold vibrator. I'd look the guys in the eye and with a naughty grin, chew on the corner of my bottom lip, bring the tool up to my mouth and kiss around its head. I'd slide this buzzing implement between my legs a few times, before rubbing it between my cleavage.

My movements would be slow, deliberate and animated. I made every effort to eke out my limited performance for as long as I could, before it got boring. That way the guys felt happy that they'd got their monies worth and would remain eager to be on their best behaviour to impress me.

During my performance, the guys would not be rubbing their thighs and dribbling as one might expect. Instead they'd be standing a polite distance away, as if they were an audience on Master-Chef. It's likely they suppressed their excitement to give their wives and partners a good servicing on their return home, but at no point did I ever fear that my performance would put my personal safety at risk. For me, there did not appear to be anything overly shocking in these events.

Strippers were regarded as a fairly respectable form of entertainment for men's gatherings. I wasn't doing anything that different from my highly regarded friends like Stella and Sadie. The no touching rules remained, but on my terms. When it felt safe and appropriate to do so, it would not be unusual for me to perch my naked body on the lap of a fully clothed, non tactile client.

I developed a few tantalising tricks with these new boobs. The implants were placed between my muscles, so with a flex of the pecs, I was able to make my boobs move in time to music if required. I'd fib, saying this wonderful skill was as a result of the many hours I spent in the gym. I would push a beer bottle between my cleavage, put my mouth around the neck of it and lean back to consume some of the contents. I'd grip a can between my breasts to hold it in place and unfasten the ring pull. If pouring the beer, I'd ask which *jug* they would like their beer from. The Aussie guys would insist on the coldest of beer. I think it must be for that reason they'd generally order middy's of beer rather than anything resembling a pint size. However, I would get a seal of approval for my beer warming service, rolling their ice cold beer cans around my boobs a few times before opening the can for them.

To cater for my new inflated chest size, I bought lots of new skimpy outfits. By now it was well into the winter season, so I adapted the outfits to give me some much needed warmth on those chilly evenings. I'd get really cold during the evenings, when I'd be walking around starkers in a clients garden, plunging my hands into ice cold water to pull out the beer cans. Yes, my nipples would be erect and skin covered with goose bumps, but not as the guys wrongly thought, because I was turned on, but because I was flipping freezing!

Elbow length gloves didn't work because they would get soaking wet, so I chopped off the hands, added fur to the cuffs and gave myself sleeves. My knee length boots gave me a little more skin covering. However, the winner was the see though long mesh cloak. I'd wear this open and occasionally flick up at the back to flash my bum. After all, they were paying to see me naked.

I remained unashamed by my job. In fact, when my mum came out to Perth to visit me for a few weeks, I took her along to one of my regular pub jobs in Rockingham. The landlord and his friends were lovely to her. She proudly looked on, watching me march back and forth behind the bar in my heels and not much else,

"Well I think it's wonderful," she commented enthusiastically,

"I wish I'd done something like you when I was your age."

I was always happy to work in areas like Rockingham or those suburbs outside of central Perth. With the lack of great wealth came a much more generous client. Those guys in the affluent areas were always tight with their cash and I suspect that's how they got to be so well off, because they didn't give it away too easily.

One of my weirdest jobs was one I got from Sadie.

"Hi Michelle, I was wondering if you would like to do a job in the next hour. It's only a couple of minutes drive from you and it's with one of my regular clients. It's just him and he just wants a girl to chat to and get his drinks," said Sadie, in her ever enthusiastic way.

"Yeah, that sounds fine, I've not done a one on one job before, but it doesn't sound a problem if you know him," I said.

"Michelle, I do need to warn you that he is a naturalist, so he'll come to the door without any clothes on. He'll be okay though, he knows the rules and he won't cause you any problems. It's two hours naked and I've told him it's two hundred, but I won't be taking any commission for this one," said Sadie.

I accepted the job because I trusted Sadie's judgement. Sure enough, he opened the door to me completely starkers. Not only did he have no clothes, he had no hair. He was completely bald of any head or pubic hair. He showed me to the fridge in the kitchen where his whisky and coke was chilling, invited me to get myself and him a drink, then ushered me to his back yard to the two sun loungers and we sat back in the midday sun, both naked.

He chatted to me about being a naturalist and that he'd go on holidays with like minded people. I told him about my line of work and stuck to my usual spiel that I worked in a bank in London, but was now back packing for the year. I told him about my love for different skimpy outfits. On his invitation, I began trying on the various outfits I had in my work bag, ranging from my leather look bondage style bikini to the see through floral baby doll nighty.

In no time my two hour nude booking was over. I'd spent most of that time clothed and seeking his opinion on the different looks. He concluded that his favourite was nude and congratulated me on my own shaven haven.

I popped my clothes back on and said goodbye. That's when it went a bit weird because he was insistent on walking me back to my car. There I was, mid afternoon, dressed in my animal print frock and platform heels, walking down the street with this completely bald, nude bloke in his Fifties. He'd linked arms with me, giving me a cheek to cheek air kiss to bid me farewell. I think his neighbours must have seen quite a bit of him, but I never saw him again.

The Coffin Cheaters were a notorious biker gang in Perth. These were the guys that were clad in their heavy worn black leather jackets, dark sunglasses and long goaty beards. For the ones that shaved their heads, they'd keep a long tail growing at the back. Voices gruff, smelling of motor oil and leather, they were always tattooed and their faces hardened by the violence they'd seen and used.

They'd book strippers and toppo waitresses to serve behind their bars. I worked at three of their club houses, all tucked away behind high fences down unassuming back streets in residential areas. They were always well mannered and polite to me, slipping their tools and knives on the bar top whilst asking for the ice cream tub containing the communal herbal cannabis. There was always a good supply of cigarettes stashed under the bar, likely to have come from some unlawful means. With heavy rock music playing, TV screens were in view of the bar area, monitoring the CCTV. cameras strategically set up around the club house and surrounding streets. They'd serve to give advanced warning should the cops be sniffing around. Little did they know that that in the real world I was a police officer. I guess that if my secret been revealed, I'd have been condemned to some horrendous experience. I heard of one girl getting a bucket of piss and shit tipped over her head for cheating on her biker boyfriend; I assume I would have had far worse. These guys loved me and I got repeat bookings, which I'd fill into my little police diary. An oversight by me, getting out such a thing in their presence. Thank God that they never noticed the police logo slapped on the front cover!

I accepted that these guys were violent criminals. Drug dealing, protection rackets, thefts and robbery were likely to be the preferred methods for the gang to make their money. However, I accepted that they were simply offering a service for which there was and probably always will be a demand. If it wasn't them, then someone else would be cashing in with such schemes. It's what makes the world go around.

I'd done the boob job and nipple piercing, but a few other bodily enhancements followed. I also had my eyeliner tattooed on. I'm aware that new less painless methods have since been developed. At that time, the tattooing involved a ninety minute process, going through absolute agony as the needle scratched its way above the eyelid, bumping over the root of each and every lash. The bottom lash line was a similar eye watering process. I had to keep my eyes open as much as possible whilst sucking on a hard boiled sweet, to attempt some distraction from the torture. It did not end there. Stepping off the beauticians chair with swollen red eyes, a second appointment was made for the top up procedure two weeks later.

Blonde hair extensions cost a fortune and took about five hours, as small clumps of synthetic hair were plaited into my own, then soldered on individually. I walked out of the salon looking like a mermaid. These flowing locks were not practical, having instructions to only wash them once a week. I felt as though I had a smelly rag attached to my head. I tolerated them for eleven weeks, before pulling the strands out myself, cracking the soldered seal with my finger tips and dragging each piece out one by one.

Pain seemed to be a common theme in my beauty regime. My second most profitable procedure (after the boob job) was a hood piercing, just above my clitoris. A body piercing studio near the train station in central Perth accommodated for this. I found myself laid out on my back on a massage bench with my legs dangling over the edge and apart. A little Oriental man with a big needle and a cotton wool bud worked his magic. I let off a little yelp as contact was made with my skin, to be told,

"I haven't done anything yet!"

It was not as painful as the nipple piercing, but was a little difficult when it came to the after care. I'd go for a wee and forget the piece of metal was there until it was too late and I'd wiped the toilet paper roughly across it . . . Ouch!

With this new feature came my new sales pitch,

"You've got me booked for two hours topless at $120, but for an extra $60, I can do the second hour nude. Before you decide, let me tell you that I have something quite beautiful and unique down there, something that is guaranteed to be very pleasing to the eye."

The deal was done and into the second hour the g-string would be removed to expose my piercing attachment . . . a pair of tiny shiny silver bells.

"Ding dong!! I'm not called Michelle My Bells for nothing. Forget the Swan Bell Tower when you have it all going on here!" I would proudly announce.

The bells were the subject of much amusement and were indeed unique. I don't think the other girls would have been crazy enough to carry off such a stunt. I liked the fact that there was nothing sexy about this and it was simply some alternative entertainment. The guys loved it and would frequently ask me to stay at their party for extended hours, getting paid of course. At times it could be tempting to stay, but I'd assess the crowd. I'd take into account how much they'd had to drink, what drugs they may have done and decide if they posed any risk to me.

There were drugs at some parties. If they were doing cannabis, then I had no major issues with that as their mood would be subdued and mellow. I almost preferred the customers when they were like that. If they were doing amphetamines then they could be a little less predictable and I didn't like that. Some of the girls did drugs. I saw some do a deal to work extra hours in exchange for drugs, which they'd take at the venue. I know Sadie didn't touch anything like that.

God, she was so straight laced, that she rarely drank alcohol and was even fearful of getting her ears pierced, let alone considering taking an illicit substance. There was no way I was getting involved in that scene. I had no need to because I was still on a life high doing such a crazy job.

With the arrival of Spring came a chock-a-block diary. During my last working week I did very well and on one day alone I worked fourteen hours. I left home at 8am, glammed up to the nines and made my way to Freemantle Sailing Club where I found Crystal Flyer, the thirty feet long yacht I was working on that day. I served the drinks, buffet snacks and chatted about nothing throughout my shift, to the small group of businessmen on their corporate outing. I was due to finish this boat trip at 4pm, but they paid extra to keep me for another hour, giving me just enough time to drive on to my next job.

This next one was for a client that had seen me in one of the pubs. He had booked Cindy and I for six hours nude. It was a long shift, but well paid considering it was worth $720. I drove into a quiet industrial estate, finding a pile of old car tyres abandoned at the side of a derelict looking building. I knew this must be the venue as cars were parked up nearby. Grungy music echoed and the smell of barbeque food emanated. Cindy's car showed up just as I was getting out and we walked around the side of the building together to meet the host. Paul, was a scruffy looking chap in his late-thirties, with an untamed beard that had bits of food stuck in it.

"Here you go girls," he said, handing over the cash as agreed.

"You'll find us a nice enough group of guys. If you have any problems, give me a shout and I'll sort it. Arh, and just to let you know, I have the really dirty girls showing up a bit later," he chuckled.

I didn't really take much notice of what Paul meant when he said about the *dirty girls* and assumed he meant that he had strippers like Sadie and Stella booked. However, it was not quite like that.

Four hours into our shift and we were feeling a little jaded, but Cindy and I reminded one another that we were well paid and we had to soldier on, keep smiling and make small talk with the now pissed up party goers. Numerous hands would dig into the peanut and crisp dishes we past around. I found it highly entertaining to give out a few facts and statistics,

"Do you know that studies show communal snacks are likely to contain microscopic particles of urine, faeces and even semen!" I warned,

"But don't worry, you can kill off the germs by alcohol consumption," I reassured.

Two ragged looking women turned up, both appearing to be in their mid to late thirties, yet likely to have been much younger, probably haggard from a heroin habit. One had short black hair and the other scruffy dyed blonde shoulder length hair. They had a little portable radio with them and twiddled with the buttons to find a music channel that went in and out of signal. They placed a picnic blanket onto the ground as the guys formed their semi circle and waited in anticipation.

This scrawny couple entered the semi circle with glazed eyes, twitchy movements and laid themselves out on the blanket, top to tail, naked. The semi circle tightened as the guys moved in for a closer look. Cindy and I remained in the wings, arm in arm, in horrified disbelief of what was taking place. These prostitutes were rubbing, grinding and wriggling around with one another. They were groaning, panting, yelping and screaming, whilst the guys watched on. We did the token round of asking the guys if they needed another beer, but they seemed too preoccupied to be drinking at that point. The distorted music was interrupted by the occasional radio advert, then fell into silence as the batteries died. The screams turned into what may have been a contented purr, but probably a snore, as the girls fell asleep on the floor and the semi circle opened up again, to the sounds of,

"Yeh, they were alright. I didn't mind watching that. I need another beer now."

A few gentle prods with a foot roused these girls, livening them up until well past midnight. They were offering up additional services in the tool cupboard. We heard that they could do a blow job for $50 and there appeared to be plenty of comings and goings from that little space. Cindy and I nervously giggled, for we were actually shocked by what was going on. However, I never felt unsafe and the guys remained polite and obedient to us, knowing that we were not *those sort of girls.*

My final job was unexpected. Daniel and I were due to be at Perth International airport for 8pm to check in for the flight back to the UK. My suitcase was packed and Daniel's beloved tools and machinery already en route via a cargo ship. That same day I was offered a 5-7 nude shift about twenty minutes drive from the airport. It was too good to turn down. I found myself for this last time getting dolled up in my heels and sparkles, with a little bit of tinsel around my waist. The bells were in position and I was coining in those final easy dollars in the warm heat of the early evening. I was making the usual small talk with the party goers, reminded that when a group of men get together, they rarely have meaningful conversations with one another and have quite a dull time in comparison to girls only parties.

I saw Sadie at that job and handed her my bag of outfits, suggesting they may be of use to some of the other girls. I drove straight to the airport where I met Daniel and a small entourage of friends bidding us farewell. I handed over the keys to my old faithful Honda Civic, which on Daniel's request I gave to his needy friend for free.

We boarded the plane and as we took off I looked out onto the twinkling lights of Perth by night. I was saddened that this marked the end of Michelle My Bells, the most amazing experience and the end of a beautiful Summer.

CHAPTER NINE

UNDER APPRECIATED

"GOOD MORNING, THIS IS *your captain speaking. We will shortly be arriving in London Heathrow, where the local time is now 9.22 am. The temperature is currently minus one with a north westerly wind."*

Grey, bleak, cold and dreary were my first impressions as we travelled in the taxi, back to my parents' home on that chilly drizzly January morning. We were in affect homeless, so I am grateful to my parents for housing Daniel and I for the very difficult three months that followed.

Within two weeks of my arrival back, I returned to work in the Police. I was posted to a station with a difficult commute. I had to do a bit of walking, driving, cycling and a train journey to get to my destination. My distant posting was apparently so as to prevent any professional problems between Neil and I. His working life remained unchanged, whilst I was castaway as far as possible. I worked the Earlies, Lates and Nights, with the ten hour shifts, along with an additional three to four hour daily travel, so this was indeed challenging. A 4.15am wake up and a 7pm arrival home were common place and absolutely knackering.

There were times when I would be so very tired during my drive home. I'd be contorting my face into various uncomfortable positions, singing as loud as I could with the windows down, necking back the Red Bull in a desperate attempt to stay awake. There were times when I'm sure I only narrowly avoided an accident, with the bump of the cats eyes in the centre of the road to re-focus my attention on driving rather than sleeping. I have no idea of statistics, nor how they would be accounted for, but I would not be surprised if tiredness was a far bigger cause of accidents than drink driving; and it was my establishment that had facilitated this situation I was now in.

I was working with a new team of colleagues. They were a great group of guys. The area I worked was rough and there was a need to remain alert and on the ball as we'd encounter plenty of hostile customers.

There I was, back in my uniform, taking statements and arresting the baddies. Little did they know that weeks earlier I'd been a stripper. There had been rumours spread to colleagues via Neil that I'd been a pole dancer. I would have loved to say that I had been, but the fact is that I'd never set eyes on a pole during my time in Australia and doubt I would have had the ability to wrap myself around one, due to lack of skill and dodgy knee joints. I noted an interest in my extended chest measurements when male colleagues took to talking to my breasts rather than my face. But this was understandable, as my boob job had been added to the topic list for the whisperers.

During my days off, I'd scan the papers and estate agents boards looking for a house to buy. House prices were steadily on the increase and with every month my banked deposit was equating to less and less equity. Daniel was far too busy to get overly involved in the house hunting. He was unwilling to look for paid work, blinkered by his unrealistic idealisation of setting up his own car restoration business, where he was sure he'd eventually make a fantastic profit. But for now, he was going to be supported by my wages alone and fund his workshop set up with much of my savings.

Daniel took an interest in one of the properties I had found. There was no chain, it was a fair price and needed some work to it, which suggested that a healthy profit could be made. However, those features were not what had gripped Daniel. But what did was his belief that this property could be adapted to have a large workshop within it. This of course was never going to happen, because I was never going to allow such a ridiculous idea and it would never meet council planning permission or approval.

By late Spring we were able to move out of my parents' house and into our new home. Daniel had never had a mortgage and with no savings, bank cards or wages of his own Daniel had a zero credit rating. This meant the mortgage was based on just my wage and was in my soul name. Daniel became a card holder for my bank account and got a business account set up, started by yet more of my savings. He found a workshop with a rather high monthly rental and council tax, but assured that he'd have this covered as he was sure to be in demand, being such a skilled professional in his trade.

The problem with Daniel was that he did not value any of the good advice that I or anyone else had to offer him.

"That's bull shit Michelle, what do you know? You don't know shit," would be his common response to the majority of my suggestions.

I was still juggling my full time shift work and commute, funding and supporting Daniel with his unrealistic goals, as well as trying to carry out work to our new home. Daniel had some big expensive ideas for this house and would spend far too much time, effort and money on simple decorating tasks. He'd seek perfection that could never be achieved on the hundred year old property.

Daniel spent hours upon hours at his workshop. He was obsessed by his non profit making business. He would occasionally return home offering me up a wad of cash, seeking my praise that he was bringing home the bacon. But that's just it, he wasn't! Yes, he was getting jobs in, but they didn't cover his outgoings nor give him a wage.

Daniel would come home smelling of oil and metal dust, which had imbedded into the pores on his face. He would rarely be dressed in anything other than his blue work overalls and slip on boots and expect me to be the perfect housewife. He'd simply collapse on the floor, prop himself up with a cushion and watch television. He continued to have appetite problems and sustained himself with milk and sweets and meat pies.

When he did occasionally drink down at our local pub, he would order his Jim Beam and Coke, offer to buy numerous other people drinks, then pay for the rounds with the bank card for my account. He continued to have the night sweats, needing to lay on an absorbent towel and blamed the anti-depressant medication for this undesirable condition. He became more thin and tired than ever and rarely appeared truly happy. Everything he did seemed to be a huge chore.

I had few friends on my return to the UK. The problem was that over the years I'd been married to Neil, we had joint friends. Once we parted those friends had to choose which team shirt they were going to wear. They could of course pick the safer option of keeping their distance from us both. In true character, Neil had been sure to bad mouth me to friends whilst I'd been away. Now that I was back home I felt ostracised.

Daniel had an arrogant manner about him. At first I'd found this character endearing, interpreting this to be an ultra confidence. However, I was now recognising this as an off putting snobbish trait which did not encourage friendships. I began to notice that many of Daniel's friends were the type that I didn't want as mine. They were the type that were likely to dabble on the wrong side of the law and had forged a friendship to get what they could from him. These acquaintances would sell him what I can only describe as rubbish. The shell of an abandoned car was one purchase. The wooden window frames from a derelict building was another. A broken old wooden kids scooter was yet another of the *antiques* which he planned to restore. These were unrealistic, unachievable projects and these items ended up being discarded as worthless after he'd spent my money to buy them.

Daniel continued to work at a loss and I finally had to refuse his further demands for cash. Although it was smacking me in the face so early on, I was stupid enough not do anything about it for quite some time, throwing good money after bad. He remained as useless as ever with regards to keeping work books, receipts and paperwork. He foolishly passed off this this requirement as "Bull-shit".

He eventually found a cheaper workshop near home, but would continue to work many hours for little financial reward. As time went on he found this demoralising, but he'd deal with it by burying his head in the sand. He'd tell others that he was a success, yet I saw no benefits to either of us.

There was many a time when I would suggest that our marriage was a sham and that we should end it. But then Daniel would become more needy then ever. I would feel sorry for him and so the vicious circle would continue, with me in effect acting as his carer rather than lover. Just as there seemed to be some uplift in his mood, something would happen to bring it back down again.

The most notable of these mood droppers was when he was the victim of a nasty unprovoked assault. He was battered by a hammer which resulted in the offender being taken to court and Daniel doing a commendable stint of giving his evidence in the box for near on two hours. The final result was that the offender was found guilty and we experienced a momentary high that justice had been done. We thought that the offender was sure to serve a spell behind bars with a suspended prison sentence already breached. However, two weeks later and a pathetic disproportionate sentence imposed, there was no imprisonment and the offender walked free to carry on life as per normal. Daniel fell into darker depression.

There were times when he'd hover around the front door a little longer than usual as he was leaving for work in the morning. He'd look me straight in the eye with a vulnerable saddened expression and say,

"Good bye Michelle."

When the evening was approaching and he still hadn't arrived home, a picture would form in my mind that he may be hanging from some beam in his work shop. I'd worry that he'd put a hose pipe into the exhaust of the car. With all these thoughts gurgling away in my mind, I'd be so relieved when I finally heard the key turn in the front door. Daniel would walk in looking worn out from his working day. I'd be willing to wait on him hand and foot, because he hadn't killed himself, not on that day.

I learnt that it's so hard to live with someone who is unwell with depression. People would ask after Daniel, knowing he'd had a bad time since the assault, yet no one asked how I was coping. My energies went on Daniel, rather than on myself. He would go into dark moods where he simply wouldn't talk, not even to enquire how my day had been. I'd ask him a question and wait patiently for a response which never came. I would interpret his silence to mean he was angry with me for no apparent reason, which became extremely frustrating. I felt I was always walking on egg shells around Daniel, who for most of the time seemed moody. He seemed to be disinterested in the fact that I still had a lot going on with my full time employment, doing up the house and having the sole responsibility of paying the bills.

It was a very lonely time for me and I desperately wanted to have affection, to be loved, cherished, adored and valued. However, I felt isolated with no one to look after me. I am fortunate that I do have a dear friend who has been there for me over the years, but she lived some distance away. It would be difficult for me to talk to her on the phone about my situation, as inevitably Daniel would be around to listen in to my phone calls. I felt trapped in my situation and needed to let off steam. I took to writing a diary where I would spill out my thoughts and feelings on paper. I found this method of self help a great tool in keeping my own sanity, allowing me to release some emotions.

'I find myself resenting Daniel for preventing me from achieving things. He's a difficult person and I can't rely on him at all. I know he starts off with good intentions, but his actions towards me, well, they're a bit crap. Tonight I came in after I'd been to Mum and Dad's. Daniel phoned at 6.20pm to say he was home and I asked him to do ironing. I came home and no ironing had been done. I knew he had no intentions of doing it or hanging out the washing that's still in the machine. Daniel was asleep with the telly on in the front room. Nothing had been done. He still smelt of work. He does that, doesn't bother cleaning himself up. When he did wake up he did bother to heat up his dinner which I'd prepared for him earlier. He couldn't really be bothered to talk too much to me. He never initiates conversation of great depth. I hate my life as it is, but any changes need loads of effort and I just don't have the energy left.'

From time to time, the focus of my thoughts and diary writings would turn to an obsession about my eating habits and calorie counting. Perhaps I was using this mindset as a distraction from the situation I was now in with Daniel. I couldn't take control of his failings, but could take control of my own. I would limit myself to 800-1000 calories a day and lose a couple of pounds. I'd feel low about my circumstances, then gain a couple of pounds and so the vicious circle went on.

'WEDNESDAY—I weighed myself tonight—11 stone, 7 pounds. So, this is it. The last chance before obesity sets in. I'm going on a detox, not a diet. This will be a pre-diet for four days. The plan for tomorrow is eat nothing. Friday is fruit and veg only. Saturday rice and veg. Sunday one egg, tuna, veg and orange. Let's see what I am on Monday morning . . . I hope less than 11 stone. The next time I will write in this diary will be Monday. If I manage this goal, then I'll achieve all my other goals . . . now there's a challenge!'

'MONDAY—The above, I stuck to it and I was eating healthily, then the days off came and on Friday I went to a leaving do, Saturday to an evening wedding reception, Sunday out for dinner and before I knew it, I'd eaten loads and not lost any weight at all. My boob has started to hurt. It feels like one of the implants is a rock. I've been reading up about it and it seems likely that I have capsular contracture, which I can do nothing about because it's scar tissue building up around the implant. The only remedy is removal and replacement. There is no way I could afford that as well as supporting Daniel at the moment. I hope something will finally go my way, there just doesn't seem any end to the uphill battles.'

Thankfully, after my many appeals to my employers, I was finally posted closer to home. This made my life a little easier as it cut down my commuting time. So, just when I thought life might be on the up, with a little more time and energy to finally devote to myself, Daniel walked in with a new addition to the home. Lucy the Border Collie arrived. Although she was cute and fluffy, I immediately recognised her as yet another time consuming responsibility, that I would no doubt be lumbered with. Indeed, this is what happened. He did not put this puppy through any training and we had virtually no garden, with just a small patch of concrete for a backyard, which was not secure. I'd be laying in bed, having got in during the middle of the night from shift work, and he'd go downstairs and get Lucy from the kitchen. Rather than doing the sensible thing of letting her out first to go for a wee, he'd send her straight up to me. So, there I was, halfway through my nights sleep, having an excited dog jumping all over me in bed. The excitement was naturally too much and Lucy would do yet another wee on the duvet or pillow. I'd start shouting at Daniel for waking me up and being so stupid to let her upstairs . . . And so my day would begin.

There would be dog hairs everywhere. Poo would be in the places you'd least expected to find it, until it was too late and it was embedded on the bottom of a shoe. Daniel simply didn't take responsibility. I tried the method of leaving the housework to build up, hoping this may insight him to finally do some. But it just didn't happen and I started to make excuses to potential visitors, because I was embarrassed at the state of the home.

I went to my doctor, a lovely lady who listened to my plight. I explained I was so worn out, tired and lacking motivation, as nothing seemed good in my life anymore and I felt I had nothing to look forward to. I said that Daniel suffered from depression and that I found it hard to deal with his illness. She fired a quick round of questions at me, encouraging immediate honest answers. It was then I realised that I'd been excusing Daniel's behaviour towards me because of his depression, but it had nothing to do with that. With or without that illness, his treatment towards me was simply unacceptable as he clearly didn't care and respect me as he should.

Events took a turn with a big family announcement from Oz. Daniel's arrogant brother John had set a wedding date. Shortly after this we got the news that Daniel's father had become very unwell. Daniel was keen to return home to be with his family at that difficult time. By extending his stay he'd be around for the wedding. And so Daniel set about his new project, arranging a four month stay in Australia. I was keen to fund this as I saw this as an opportunity to get some respite from his depression and to be myself for a while. I encouraged him make his trip as long as he needed it to be. I felt that his escape from yet another of our British winters, may lift his spirits and with luck improve his health. In his own mind, he could finally justify closing the doors on his metal work business, end the rental on the workshop and put his tools into storage. With another trip to Heathrow Airport and an emotional goodbye, he was gone, for now.

From the moment Daniel departed, my life went on the up and I turned from recluse to socialite. Once free of Daniel, I felt strong enough to finally tell him I did not want him in my life anymore. However, he did not leave graciously and attempted to fleece me for yet more money through solicitors. He had unrealistic expectation that because he had been my husband, be it for a short time, that he was now entitled to half of everything I owned. He even expected some sort of future allowance from my pension. Unfortunately, as ridiculous as his demands were, because he was making them, the dispute had to go through the courts. All of this was costing me yet more money. I was left feeling that all I'd ever done for him and all I'd ever given had been completely dismissed and under valued. Financially, the end result was that he got nothing extra than I'd already generously given him. Yet I was left with a solicitors bill running into thousands of pounds. At that time that money could have been better spent on something purposeful.

CHAPTER TEN

SCANDALOUS

I'D ALREADY BEEN PRESCRIBED Prozac for a few months. However, it wasn't until Daniel finally left that my mind and body went into protest mode. I'd been something of a carer to Daniel for so long. Emotionally, I was simply burnt out. Now that there was no need for me to devote my energies to Daniel, I only had myself to think of. My inner spirit was screaming out that it needed some rest and recuperation from the previous unsettling three to four years.

I now found that I had so little motivation. I would quite happily stay in bed all morning. I'd surfaced sometime after midday, then I'd spend the first part of the afternoon in my pyjamas before finally getting dressed half way through the day. I would liken the experience to walking through syrup, every moment of the day. I couldn't concentrate that well. I'd be in the middle of a task then forget what I was doing and couldn't shake myself back into reality. I'd have to write myself out little sticky notes to remind myself of the simplest of tasks to be done. I felt I had fallen down a deep dark hole of doom and gloom, that I had managed to scramble up some way, and was getting closer to the daylight. However, I was not quite there yet and feared I may slip and fall deeper down again.

I still had no proper heating in the home, so would light the open fire and huddle up to it. I'd love those evenings when I was home alone with the fire blazing and music playing. Snacking on a packet of crisps and opening a bottle of Shiraz, I'd feel mellow from a few glasses of red. I'd have the phone beside me and chat for hours to friends, as if they were in the same room with me. Although on my own, this was the first time in ages when I didn't feel at all lonely.

The doctor signed me off work with depression and referred me for a course of counselling. This was now a time for me to take stock of my life, look back and reflect. I began to realise that my kind caring nature had not always worked well for me. I'd describe it this way, that if I was with a group of people and a variety of cakes was offered, I would wait until everyone else had selected their choice and settle with whatever cake remained. I'd politely have the least popular cake, even if it was one I didn't even like. I'd do that so that everyone else was okay. I knew I had to break this cycle and put myself first for a change. I started using the fake tan again, putting a bit of sparkle in my make-up and buying some new clothes and CD's. I had to convince myself that I was entitled to put myself first and buy things for me and me alone, rather than feeling I should restrict such things as a rare treat.

When I heard a social event was taking place, I now made every effort to be there. Often it took me most of the day to prepare and motivate myself to attend. I was on my own and realised the importance of social interaction at this time of recovery. There can be a stigma attached to being off work with depression, an expectation that you should be at home crying all day long and if you're not then to everyone else you look perfectly well. You have no sling or bandage to show off. I'm sure that colleagues were passing judgement when they saw me on yet another night out in a local pub, appearing to have a great time skiving off work. It always worked out that during those rare moments when I'd managed to motive myself to get out there for a short jog, the police van would be passing just as I was in the middle of an energetic sprint. A battle with my conscience would follow, where I'd feel as if I was letting my colleagues down and that I should return to work regardless of my mental health problems.

As I went out more, I got to meet new people through friends of friends. I was open about my recovery from depression. Such openness and honesty appeared to be endearing enough to others, as they revealed their own insecurities and that they too struggled with their mental health. So many of my new friends confessed to being on anti-depressants themselves. Being around such people made me feel accepted and that I wasn't so different after all.

Three of the most notable characters were Gemma, Vicky and Ryan. Their employment involved looking after others, displaying strong character traits of being kind, caring and genuine. All three had been friends for years and had a unique bond. They would say little one liners that would clearly remind them of some previous experience and send them into a fit of giggles. All three were attractive in their own ways, but Vicky was the outstandingly pretty one. She was tall with long, straight blonde hair, big blue flirty eyes and long dark lashes that would flutter as she listened intently to whatever was being told to her, before smiling to flash off her perfectly straight white teeth.

Gemma had an enthusiastic entertaining presence about her. On her arrival at an event, she was sure to liven it up. She had been overweight for years and once confessed to eating a jar of peanut butter in the same way that anyone else would eat a yoghurt. The thing with Gemma was that she was so sexy with her presentation and personality that her weight seemed insignificant. She always wore the most flattering clothing and her make-up was to perfection. Her hairstyles ever changing, being twisted and turned into various creations, with the odd hair piece being fixed in place. If she'd been born a male, then she would have been a drag queen, with her flamboyant styles. With Gemma, it was her warmth, personality, singing voice, laughter and mere presence that was larger than life.

Ryan had moulded into this friendship as a previous work colleague of Gemma's. She'd fancied the pants off him, only to be eternally disappointed after Ryan confessed that he could never remotely be attracted to her at all. He was gay. Ryan, AKA Bungle Bonce had thick short dark hair, with a good lashing of product to mould it into what ever the chosen style be for the day. A Mohican, quiff or perhaps a spiky boy band crop. A dedicated follower of fashion, he'd come up with a few trends of his very own. Cutting two pairs of trousers in half and sewing them together at the crutch and arse, proudly modelling a pair of jeans from the left side and chinos to the right. Ryan would wear his cheeky smile, reminding us girls that it was okay to get changed and naked in front of him, because he was after all, gay. Once we were dressed, he'd warmly grace us with a comment such as,

"Babe, you look amazing!"

My new found friends made me feel proud that I was actually very normal. Together we were open with one another about our failings and insecurities, but at the same time we reminded each other about our strengths and achievements. We all felt we'd been through the mill a bit, we'd all taken or were taking anti-depressants and together we boarded a roller coaster ride of fun, adventure and excitement.

We'd all make an effort to go out to do fun things. We'd go for trips to London to stay in a posh hotel and go to a night club, somewhere like G.A.Y or Heaven. Or we'd get together for a picnic in the park. A couple of my dearest oldest friends joined the ride and for the first time in ages I found that I was truly laughing. I might suddenly let off a little giggle at random moments in the day, when something had pinged into my head of a funny event or a stupid thing that had happened to one of us during a night out, when we'd had a little too much to drink. It was a good feeling to finally have.

The nights out were good and I found that with the medication, I'd only need one glass of wine to feel merry, so I was a cheap night out! The best part was getting ready to go out, followed by returning home with sore dancing feet, getting changed into fleecy pyjamas and enjoying a cup of milky tea and buttery toast.

My spacious home became the party house. I had little in the way of good furniture or possessions to be overly precious about, so if a drink did get spilt, then it was no drama and could easily be wiped up. The karaoke machine would come out and Gemma would entertain us with her singing talents, whilst Vicky and I would do micky take pole dancing attempts. There was plenty of room for guests to stay over if need be and the best part was the de-brief the following morning. Gemma, Vicky and Ryan would gather on the bed beside me as we'd unpicked the events of the previous evening. We'd giggle at the silly things we'd all done. Reminiscing at just how much fun we'd had.

Of course, the whispers would follow from the people who'd not been invited to the party and we'd crack up at the suggestions that our gatherings at home were in fact wild swingers' parties. I can confirm that there were no car keys in hats, not a swing in sight and to date, the only married men I've ever shagged are the ones I've been married to! My mum attended most of my house parties to entertain us with her crystal ball, reflexology foot massages and hand readings, so she is was my witness! I'd led a somewhat boring life with Daniel and now these rumours made my life sound exciting, so I did little to quash them.

With my new found enthusiasm for fun seeking, along with my official single status (be it separated, waiting for divorce), I re-discovered my sexual confidence. My weight remained the same as ever, yet was of little importance to me now, because I believed that I was truly beautiful and felt attractive to others. I loved standing out in a crowd and would thrive on being the centre of attention. I'd deliberately wear clothing to be noticed and embraced a rock chick image. I'd be wearing one of my many see-through mesh tops with a sparkly silver bra on show underneath. I'd wear brightly coloured clothing and would always seek to overdress for any occasion.

If I could shock others, then as far as I was concerned, that was brilliant! I was finally being noticed again. Gemma shared this tactic and we found it hilarious to be in the centre of a dance floor in a crowded nightclub, whilst others stood back in disbelief as we shared a full on snogging session with one another. It was around that time that I began to question why I should limit my sexual availability exclusively to men, when all I'd experienced was losers. There were a lot of attractive people out there and some of them just happened to be female. I decided to explore lesbianism.

I was a little unsure where to begin with this new exploration. I started by openly voicing that I was questioning my sexuality. One of my lesbian colleagues was very sweet about my curiosity, popping by with a pile of gay/lesbian magazines for me to flick through. In these magazines was the lesbian and gay switchboard telephone number. After giving it a call, I was contacted by Lisa, a local representative. She explained that a group met at a local pub every other week and invited me along.

On my arrival outside the Duke of York pub, I had no problems identifying Lisa. She was a short lady in her late forties, doing nothing to show off her slim figure. Instead she chose to wear a pair of baggy blue jeans and oversized denim jacket. Her hair was short, mousy brown with grey flecks running through and she wore no make-up. Lisa was brilliant. She instantly took me under her wing and introduced me to the other girls. They were a mixed bunch by way of their age and attractiveness. They chatted about the various social events attended and forthcoming. The ones that had them, spoke of their partners just like anyone else. They were grumbling about something they hadn't done and praising them for what they had. I did however struggle with the concept that some of these girls were butch, just as Lisa was. Some of these boyish girls had the most feminine beautiful partners and I just didn't get what these attractive girls would see in the butch ones. Should us women not embrace our femininity and love our girlyness, wanting to wear dresses, make-up and play with our hair?

I noticed that these girls did not appear to be seeking out a casual fling. They were searching for love and commitment, which was not at all on my agenda.

It was at one of these lesbian social events that I met Heather, aged in her mid-twenties. She was slim, attractive and had an almost innocent presence about her, with her porcelain skin and long curly auburn hair. She invited me back to her sparsely furnished home, explaining that she'd only recently moved in. I opened a bottle of wine and as we sipped on our drinks and chatted, I got the impression that she was not an accustomed wine drinker like myself, as her glass was not going down quite as quickly as mine.

Her tiny home had just the one bedroom and as we went into her room, a single bed was pushed against the wall with a tiny cross hanging above the pink valour padded headboard. We slipped our clothes off and snuggled under the duvet, where I felt her soft skin touch mine. Everything about intimacy with a woman felt so different from being with a man. There was no abrasive rough stubbled face nor pent up eagerness to deliver. My girl on girl experiences were soft skinned, sweet smelling, gentle, slow, intense and most of all fun. Heather was all those things. However, concern, bordering on horror engulfed me as she wrapped her arms around me, covered me in kisses and somewhat tearful declared,

"Michelle, I love you, never leave me!"

I appreciate for us girls, with our hormones, emotions and all that, sometimes get overwhelmed at times like these. It can be enough for any guy to grab his stuff and do a runner immediately. For a brief moment, I wanted to do that guy thing, but I felt I needed to take responsibility. So, I gently stroked her hair, assured her it was okay to *love the moment*, until she fell asleep. I had been drinking, so had no choice but to stay the night. I left the following morning and never saw dear Heather again.

I did however see lots of other women. When I chatted to straight girls about my experiences, many would confess that they were bi-curious and invite me to help them out with their curiosity. Dare I say it, these girls were practically throwing themselves at me. They were all gorgeous and fun to be with, but I still fancied guys too.

Of course, telling my male acquaintances that I had the occasional girlfriend seemed to encourage them even more. So with that came a plentiful supply of fit guys. I was now independent and happy in my own company, yet when I needed the physical contact, it was plentiful. There were of course times when Ryan, Vicky and Gemma would perch themselves on my bed and suggest that my conquest of the previous evening had not been that fit.

"Was it the beer goggles darling?" questioned Vicky.

"Oow, cheeky! He, he, he!," mocked Gemma.

"You were doing charity that night weren't you babe?" suggested Ryan.

It didn't seem quite so bad that I'd shared an intimate moment with a 5/10 scoring stranger, if it was a charitable gesture. Rather that than calling it a drunken misjudgement. It sustained my physical needs, but what of the emotional needs? Well that's just it, I didn't feel I had any. The Prozac seemed to have suppressed my emotions and I began to wonder if this was healthy to sustain.

I went back to my doctor and discussed my mental health and Prozac use. I went to counselling and was offered a week long stay at the police rehabilitation centre. During my service I'd paid a monthly subscription to the welfare fund, which allowed officers to apply for a stay at the home when needed. It was during my stay at the home that I reflected on my past experiences and thought long and hard about my future aspirations.

Although it was fun for the short term, I didn't want to continue with meaningless liaisons for the long haul. They had been entertaining and I certainly didn't feel guilty about my temporary promiscuous behaviour. It was socially acceptable for single guys to behave the way I had been and get praised for their conquests. I was still in my early-thirties and still hoped that Mr Right was out there somewhere for me. I dreamed that we'd get married, have lots of babies and live happily every after.

During my stay at the rehabilitation centre, I met police officers that had been through some horrific experiences and suffered some terrible injuries. As I chatted to the various temporary residents, I met Matt over a game of Bingo. As he held a pen to quickly cross off his numbers during the game, I spotted his racing, pulsating wrist. He was clearly taking this game very seriously. He appeared to be the leader on his team table, arranging for the whip for the next round of drinks and generously contributing just a little extra so that the rounds were well covered.

We established that we'd coincidently grown up in the same village and attended the same school. Matt stood out from the others that I met there. He was tall, ruggedly handsome and muscular. He stood at over six feet tall, with a broad frame, tanned complexion and a deep gentle tone in his voice. I could hear his voice over all the others, as I subconsciously searched him out in a crowded room, whether it be in the dining hall, sports area or bar.

I really liked him. I didn't own a mobile phone at that time, so gave him a landline number, yet never heard back from him. Once I was back at work I tracked him down via e-mail. I sent a little message wishing him well and forwarding a new mobile number. Some weeks later, out of the blue, he called me!

Matt and I began casually seeing each another. He was still in and out of a relationship and I was going through my court battle with Daniel. Matt and I lived some distance apart, so we'd arrange to meet at a midway point and go somewhere nice. We might stay in a hotel, go to a West End show or out for a nice meal. We'd have a great time and I'd look forward to our next date.

But Matt was a hard cookie to crumble and seemed hesitant to commit to me alone. I would have my doubts about him when he'd say he didn't know what he wanted and tell me he planned to keep his options open. We'd chat on the phone and he'd mention that a girlfriend had asked him to marry her. I'd pass his comments off by offering to be a bridesmaid, but deep down I worried that he was stringing me along. For that reason, I continued to date other men, so that I didn't get too emotionally attached. But it was hard, because Matt was always in my thoughts. I wrote in my diary a text message I wanted to send him, but never did.

'Matt, I really adore your company and would love you to be in my life more and more . . . but I am also learning self preservation! I recognise that you are juggling your women about and keeping all options open, which is fair game, definitely. But I don't want to make myself vulnerable, so don't want to play that game and will have to leave you to it. Sorry, good Luck, M x'

It was early summer when Matt and I spent an amazing weekend together in London. During our journey back home he told me he didn't want to say goodbye to me any more. He was willing to uproot and move in with me. And so, that's what happened. Some months later, my diary entry read,

'I love Matt to bits. He makes me feel safe, cared for, valued and respected. He has helped so much to motivate me to make my house a home. He is so encouraging and made me a better person. I can't imagine life without Matt. He tells me I am gorgeous and I feel adored by him. He is the best!'

Although Matt had moved in with me, a change of events at work meant I was posted to a station closer to Matt's former home. So for a time we lived between our two properties, staying at his place during the working week, then returning to my house during the days off. It was a challenging time and the whisperers were wrongly convinced that my forced work move was due to my many swingers parties. They thought that my life was simply far too scandalous for me to remain where I was. I was once again feeling ostracised. But I could deal with it this time around, because Matt believed in me. He was a huge support at a time when I could have been pushed out of my job for good.

I gushed with happiness. We both did. As we lay in bed, we talked about our future. We spoke of how wonderful it would be to have our baby laying between us. We'd be a family, united and happy. There could see no reason why we shouldn't take the step to try for our very own brood. After all, I was reaching my mid-thirties and wanted to have lots of children. I thought four would be a good number, just as my own parents had achieved. We were in a home that was large enough to house a family and even an au-pair if need be. There was a crèche and Primary School just up the road and my parents would be available to help with child care. It seemed like a great idea!

And so the baby making attempts began. I was checking my diary, counting the days and working out the date when I would be most likely to conceive. After the first month there was no joy, the second month felt different and I thought this may be it, but it wasn't. The third month came and went, but during the fourth month events took a turn that changed our plans forever.

Chapter Eleven

I TURN TO YOU

After a challenging couple of months, I was posted to my old station. The journey to work was still fairly long, but it was a commute that Matt and I could do together, so it was far more tolerable.

We moved back to my house full time and continued with our plans to have children. We even spoke of names. A girl was to be named Meghan and a boy would be called Maximus, after the film Gladiator. With a name like that he was sure to be strong and successful. By now, I smoked very little, perhaps a couple of cigarettes a day at most and I had a healthy diet. We both did.

It was my third day at the new station and I was posted on plain clothes patrol. During that evening shift I ate my sandwiches, but kept feeling like I had indigestion. I thought I needed to burp or maybe have a good fart. Perhaps the discomfort was due to the positioning of my hefty utility belt concealed under my clothing. The pain wouldn't go away and as the end of my shift approached, I felt unable to get going with my journey back home, which started with a bike ride.

I thought I'd wait a little longer for the discomfort to pass. I moved around a bit, bent my body into different positions, hoping this trapped wind feeling would release. But it wouldn't. It just got gradually worse until I was huddled on the sofa in the rest room at the station. I felt embarrassed that I was appearing to my new colleagues to be some drama queen.

"*Well . . .*" said Sergeant Knowles,
"*I'm making the decision for you. You're going to hospital to get checked out and Gavin is going to take you.*"

I hardly knew PC Gavin Ford. But within the hour, he was my companion in the busy hospital A&E department waiting area, as I commenced the five hour wait to be seen by the doctor. My on-duty PC status and extreme pain didn't allow for a queue jumping privilege. So, I waited in line with the smelly drunks who'd had a fight or fallen over in yet another drunken stupor. They were seen before me. I was given some pain killers, but I brought them up within minutes of taking them. By the time Matt arrived to take over from PC Ford, I was wracked with a relentless pain. No matter what I did, what position I contorted myself into, the pain did not hold off. Not even for a brief moment. It just got worse. We have spoken about this since and for Matt it was a distressing time, because he felt completely helpless and was unable to be my protector and take the pain away.

When I was finally seen by the doctor, they questioned whether I could be pregnant and perhaps experiencing an ectopic pregnancy. Although I really tried, the immense pain rendered me unable to give even a dribble of a urine sample. Matt held my hand and stayed with me as I was injected with morphine. I was so worn out from the pain. Although I appeared calmer, the effect of the morphine was minimal because I was still just as riddled with horrendous pain. I was just physically unable to complain so much about it.

The next moment I remember was waking up and Matt had gone. I was in a hospital ward that smelt of urine and old ladies. I had a drip tube attached to my hand. I was feeling very sleepy and still in and out of consciousness. I could hear the sounds of the nurses chatting on handover and tuned in more intensely when I heard my name.

"Michelle is at bed three. She's still asleep. She has had a fallopian tube removed . . ."

Whatever else those nurses were saying I didn't hear it, because it resounded in my head,

"fallopian tube removed, fallopian tube removed."

My heart sunk to my stomach and I suddenly felt very alert and awake.

"Oh my God!" I thought, *"If I have just the one fallopian tube, then it's so much more difficult to get pregnant."*

I felt overwhelming disappointment. This could not have come at a more unwanted time, when we are trying for a child. Okay, I know that many women go on to have families with just one fallopian tube in operation. But life had been difficult enough of late and I just wanted something to go to plan for once.

I scrambled around and found a call button to summons over a nurse, who came within moments.

"I've just heard you talking," I sobbed. *"I heard you say I'd had my fallopian tube removed. That's terrible. We're trying for a family."*

The nurse could say nothing of comfort and said she would arrange for someone to come to speak with me about the operation. Sometime later a doctor arrived at my bedside.

"When we commenced your operation, we discovered the reason for your pain was a twisted fallopian tube. We had to cut it away and found the other was also damaged and full of fluid that needed to be released. We had to cut the other tube. Although it remains in your body, it is no longer able to operate as it should. I hear that you have been trying for children, but your only chance of this will now be though IVF treatment. You will not be able to get pregnant naturally."

I was now in total shock, for the facts were far worse than I'd initially thought. They were unimaginably worse. This was simply a revelation that I was completely unprepared for. No definitive reason was given for my condition, but it was suggested that the most likely cause was damage by the sexually transmitted disease, Chlamydia. Tests did not indicate that I currently had such a condition, but I thought back to my visit to the GUM clinic some years earlier. I recalled the diagnosis of Chlamydia at that time and the unknown damage that had already been done. It seemed that although Neil had long since been removed from my life, his legacy remained with me.

When Matt came into the ward I was distraught as I began to tell him that I had some unimaginable, terrible news to break to him. He squeezed my hand as I blurted out that I would never be able to naturally give him the children we had dreamed of. Tears rolled down his cheeks as he exhaled an almightily breath of relief, throwing me into momentary confusion,

"You daft cow! I thought you were going to tell me you were going to die!" sobbed Matt, *"I couldn't bear losing you. A child would be wonderful. An extension of my love for you. But it is not the be all and end all. You are the most important thing to me. We can work through it. We can succeed!"*

Inside I was feeling like a failure, that everything feminine about me was infected and removed. I felt like a reject. Unable to give the love of my life something that he really wanted. A child. Yet Matt's words served as overwhelming comfort of acceptance at that difficult time. He remained with me until I fell back to sleep, still heavily dosed up with medication and all unattractiveness uncovered. My labia was swollen to the size of testicles and was purple in colour. I had an uncomfortable catheter tube connected to a piss bag hooked to the side of the bed, unexplained bruising on my torso and various wires and bleeping machines surrounding me. After five nights in the hospital, I was released with a pile of iron tablets to combat anaemia. This helped to explain why I'd been feeling so tired of late.

I always assumed that I would be able to have children. After all, I'd been to Egypt, running round the Scarab beetle three times to endorse my fertility! I'd never had any need to research the term IVF in the past. As far as I knew, it was simply something to do with babies being grown in a test tube and what happened to other people, not me.

Three months later we attended an appointment with a fertility doctor and it was then that I began to establish that the IVF process was a lengthy journey. We could not even begin to start the process unless we funded it ourselves. Before we went down that route, my remaining damaged fallopian tube needed to be removed. In its current condition, an implanted embryo could travel up the tube. The doctor said statistics showed that younger people were more likely to be successful with IVF treatment. Delays simply lessened our chances of success. The fallopian tube operation was available on the NHS, but I was told that the waiting list may be lengthy. He suggested private treatment at £1500, could speed up the process. We left agreeing with the doctor that private treatment was the way we should go and he gave instructions about his private clinic and how to book the operation. He said this could be done within a four week period. Nothing would be confirmed until payment was received.

On our return home, Vicky, a nurse herself, was keen to know how our appointment had gone. I relayed the explanation given by the doctor about NHS waiting times and his recommendation to go private. She offered some valuable advice.

"Look, Michelle, it's up to you what you both do, but £1500 is a lot of money, especially when you think about the future expense you are likely to have with IVF. The NHS is currently monitored for their waiting list times and you may not find you have to wait that much longer for the operation. You pay

all that money in National Insurance payments towards the health service, so you deserve something back from it."

We took Vicky's advice and within six weeks I was back in hospital having my remaining fallopian tube removed courtesy of the NHS. Step one was complete and the next stage was to apply for funding for the IVF process. I began my research and intently read the newspaper articles. Reports from the Human Fertilisation and Embryology Authority (HFEA) recommend that every local Primary Care Trust offer three funded treatments to couples. I read about Post Code Lotteries on this subject and despite the recommendations, some Trusts only offered one treatment to infertile couples.

I was directed to my GP to establish what I would be offered. Even though neither Matt or I had children and there was absolutely no chance whatsoever of me getting pregnant naturally, my Trust did not see this as a priority. They chose to decline any funding to couples like us. The GP said that funding was under review. Even if one treatment was paid for, it would be to a female aged thirty-six or over, who had never had IVF before. At that time I was thirty-four. I was told that by the age of thirty-six, chances of success deplete and that one complete IVF cycle would cost around £5000.

I'd heard that many couples needed numerous IVF cycles. If we were to have funded an attempt ourselves and it failed, we'd never have be entitled to any future funding. We thought long and hard and decided to put any plans on hold. I have no doubt that this was the right decision at that time.

Chapter Twelve

MY LOVE FOR YOU, INSATIABLE

Work Hard, Play Hard. This seemed to be the common theme that followed for the next couple of years. With military precision, the alarm would be set for 4.45am and we'd be out of the door no later than 5.15am. This would enable us to meet our travel connections and in just under an hour into our joint travel, we'd bid one another a good day, then continue our separate ways to our places of work, ready for our 7am start. Once the working day was coming to a close, we'd text each other to see if there were going to be any delays, perhaps if we had a prisoner in custody or a job that was going to take some time. All being well, we'd meet at the set time and place, ready for our joint commute home.

The late shifts were a bit more tricky as public transport was not so plentiful in the middle of the night. But this was a joint operation and we were successful at it. During our journey home we'd give a debrief of our working day. We'd chat about the tossers we'd encountered, the demands we'd been stretched to and the thankless tasks we'd completed. By the time we got home, we were all done with talking about the job. PC Matt and WPC Michelle were boxed away until another day and we were free to relax and be ourselves.

I used to find that after an early shift, by the time we got home, we were both shattered and would do little more than collapse in front of the TV to catch up with the soaps. It was the hours after the late shifts that I enjoyed the most. Lates would generally be the most demanding of shifts. By the time we got home, it was the early hours of the morning. By then we felt more than deserving of a bottle of wine . . . Each.

I loved the sound of *'pop'*, followed by *'glug, glug, glug, glug, glug'* (which from experience amounts to sufficient glug's to fill one glass). The predictable night time TV would commence. Semi clad girls with plastic boobs and synthetic hair would suggest we phone them on a premium rate number as they were desperate to get our call. We'd flick channels to see a presenter with a stick on smile, beckoning us to purchase really useful household products because it could change our lives forever. We were never sucked into any of this, but it kept us entertained as we sipped on the wine and felt the release of the tensions from the previous day.

We talked and talked and loved one another's company. Our time off together during rest days was very valuable to us. We'd plan our next adventure, talk about potential holiday destinations and thrive on the thrill of arranging City Breaks. We'd go online, scan Expedia and Lastminute.com for the best deals and book a three night European trip to locations such as Prague, Berlin and Rome. We had a few friends in London and would get busy making arrangements to visit them during yet another theatre trip.

Sometimes, just sometimes, we'd exchange the night-time TV for a couple of brushes and a pot of paint, determined to get a few walls decorated before we went to bed. Our home became a project and we were keen to get it looking fabulous. It was around that time that the financial dispute instigated by Daniel was finalised in court. This meant the Caution on my property was removed and I was finally able to release some equity in my home by re-mortgaging. The money then went towards the home improvements project, much of it done by ourselves. It was lovely that although Matt had moved into my house, he was now able to put his own mark on the place to make it feel like his home too.

We loved entertaining and would make any excuse to throw parties for our friends. I'd get busy in the kitchen by baking fresh bread. I have no idea why bread making machines were invented, when it's so easy to do from scratch. I'd make up a legendary curry and perhaps knock up a few cup cakes for good measure. The party punch was a joint effort as we tipped in the remaining dregs from the spirit bottles we had lurking in the cupboard for far too long. We'd add a good helping of vodka, some cheap white wine, chuck in the tropical fruit juice, a splash of red food colouring, artificial sweetener, chopped up fruit and we were done. I have no idea of the alcohol content, nor the quantity of unhealthy E numbers, but no one was complaining.

The karaoke machine would be back out and I would start the show by bellowing out that Alison Moyet power ballad, All Cried Out, followed by Matt and his heart felt, yet vocally strained version of Insatiable by Darren Hayes. The words he sung were for me and me only.

"We never sleep we're always holding hands, kissing for hours, talking, making plans. I feel like a better man. Just being in

the same room. We never sleep, there's just so much to do. Too much to say, can't close my eyes when I'm with you. Insatiable, the way I'm loving you."

If Matt was on a roll, then he'd go straight into Daniel Beddingfield's love song, serenading me with the lines,

"If you're not the one then why does my soul feel glad today? If you're not the one then why does my hand fit yours this way? . . . If you're not the one then why do I dream of you as my wife?"

After that, it would be a battle for the microphone as our party guests entertained all with those tunes they only ever previously sung alone in the privacy of their car, helped along by the radio.

Now, our parties were not exclusively for karaoke fans. We wanted all of our guests to feel involved and would invite the non singers to play a little something on one of my wooden recorders, or provide the percussion for one of the singers with the shaking of a tambourine. They may instead choose to read a poem or perform a party trick to match mine. I'd demonstrate that I could make my boobs move without touching them, then commence flexing my pecs just like I did in Australia, this time clothed of course! Others would follow, demonstrating that they could touch their nose with their tongue or fold their eye lids upwards. And so we'd fall into a fit of giggles and the merriment would roll on.

At that time, my brother and his wife were living in a trendy part of London. They had no kids and were always up for a night on the town. So we'd jump at the chance to visit them. During one such visit they declared that they had an announcement to make.

"Rachel has been to the doctors today and we've had it confirmed," said my brother Steve. *"Rachel is pregnant!"*

For a brief moment, I felt numbness. Even now I scorn myself as I recall my instant thought was *"How unfair, why is she pregnant and not me?"*

I pray that I gave no inkling of my selfish instinctive reaction. I wore a huge smile, and declared,

"That's wonderful news. How exciting. I'm finally going to be an Auntie!"

As Steve and Rachel went into details about the due date, where they planned to have the baby, how morning sickness had been and the potential of pregnancy cravings, I had time to remove my selfish thoughts and be genuinely interested in the forthcoming event.

My family were clearly on a roll, because within weeks of this announcement, my little sister Abby, declared that she too was pregnant. Although this pregnancy had come as something of a surprise, she was to get married to her partner before the birth. This second birth announcement thankfully filled me with no selfish thoughts, as I seemed more prepared. I reminded myself that I too could have children in the future with the assistance of IVF. After all, I still had the ovaries. I simply lacked the transport within my body to get the egg to the womb.

Matt and I were a pair of socialites. If there was a party or event to attend then we'd make every effort to be there. If the party was some distance away, then we'd stay in a hotel. Sometimes we'd get to the accommodation early so we could check in to drop off our things. We'd then head off for lunch, go shopping for a new outfit to wear to the party and pick up a little gift for the host. During that time, there were a few weddings to attend and we all love a good wedding. We'd take note of what had or had not worked for the day and made suggestions of how we'd do things if it was our wedding.

Matt never proposed marriage to me. In fact, I've been married three times, yet never experienced that down on one knee marriage proposal. However, we just seemed to know that we wanted to be together forever and it seemed a natural progression to get married. And so, we set about arranging our wedding. Matt had always spoken enthusiastically about Jamaica. He'd been on a holiday there and hoped it could one day be his wedding destination. With a visit to a travel agent, we found his Jamaican dream could be a reality. We had friends that were keen to join us for our wedding abroad, so we set about the arrangements.

Never did I think that I'd find myself on wedding number three by the time I was in my mid-thirties. But there I was, having done the church with meringue dress wedding the first time and the registry office wedding the second time around. The beach venue was set as my third and final wedding. The beauty with this one was that it was inexpensive compared with a traditional wedding. The usual lengthy planning and preparation was taken out of our hands because a set wedding package was offered by the travel company. This included flowers, cake, photographer, video and legal documentation.

We arrived in Jamaica a week before our wedding and arrival of our guests. We felt that our early arrival would allow as to have a week out in the sun, to get ourselves tanned and beautiful, so that we'd looked bronzed for the photographs. In reality, the harsh sun had turned us a slightly blotched red colour, but nothing was going to ruin our special day, one which I will never forget.

We chose a 5pm wedding, which gave us a day together on the beach with our friends. At about 3pm, I said my farewells and headed back to the hotel room to begin beautifying myself. Being transatlantic, the electricity voltage was not compatible with my hair straighteners, so I chose a slightly wavy look for my bridal hair. My wedding dress was an off white, with a faint beige leaf pattern shimmering through, embellished with tiny pearls. It hung straight to the ground, but flicked out at the bottom. The cowl neckline hung low and the multiple straps on the shoulders criss-crossed at the back. As I slipped this dress on, I could feel the lining sticking to my clammy skin from the heat of the day. A cluster pearl necklace donned my neck and a little sparkly tiara glistened in my hair.

As I walked out to the waterfront, I wore a smile from ear to ear. Matt stood proudly in a stone coloured suit and beaded necklace, beside the ornate wedding arch, decorated with pink and white flowers. Ronan Keating's ballad played out as I walked down the path towards my soon to be husband.

"If tomorrow never comes, will she know how much I loved her?"

There we were, with our gathering of friends and family, beside the beautiful blue Jamaican waters. It was just as the sun was setting and its deep orange glow reflected against the ripples on the sea. We looked into each other's eyes, declaring that we took one another as husband and wife. As we held hands, saying our vows, I just about managed to hold back an emotional outburst of happiness. I felt elated that after some trial and error, I had finally found my Mr Right.

Cake cutting and a few short speeches followed. As the evening set in, we all sat out by the waters edge, dining on fine food and champagne. Our chosen selection of love songs played subtly in the background. The festivities continued throughout the week, because in effect we were now on the honeymoon period, surrounded by our nearest and dearest.

Marriage made little difference to us. We were as happy before marriage as we were afterwards. One of the factors for marriage was that we wanted our future child/children to be within wedlock, so as to show a united bond and be a traditional proper family.

On our return from Jamaica, we got the fantastic news that we'd been accepted for a work posting much closer to home. We'd still be working the same shifts as one another and have an extra couple of hours a day free from commuting. We'd save the expense of travel fares and I would have time to go to the gym.

I was keen to get myself into peak fitness in preparation for our future IVF plans. A shocking front page headliner in a tabloid newspaper splashed the words, *'Smoking just one cigarette a day is detrimental to fertility.'* I decided there and then to pack up. There was no weaning myself off gradually or wearing nicotine patches. That revelation alone was enough to motivate me to kick the habit and I've not looked back since.

We were fully aware that if we were to have a family, then our lifestyle was soon to change dramatically. There would be no more guaranteed lavish annual holidays and no spur of the moment City Breaks. So, we set about planning a holiday of a lifetime.

We set off for a five week holiday to Australia, with a stop-over either side of the journey. Tommy was there to meet us from Perth airport and drove us around some of my old haunts such as Neil Hawkins Park to see the Kangaroos and Kookaburras at dusk. We went to Hillary's, where years earlier I'd go for the all you can eat menu deal at The Jetty. This time we went to the more up market Portafino's restaurant. The Swan Bell Tower was still in the process of being built when I was last there, but it now stood in its full glory beside the river, offering fantastic views over the city from the tower.

A few days later we went on to stay with Sadie and Cole. They'd arranged a fun packed itinerary, which included a visit to the peaceful Rottnest Island where we cycled and met the Quokkas. We were shocked to hear that these cute furry creatures were known to be victims of Quokka Soccer by the occasional drunken yob. Sadie had pre-booked beach side accommodation at Yallingup, in the Margaret River region. We went on the entertaining Winery Tour, and Cole cheekily treated us by flashing his arse off in most of our photographs.

During our trip to Australia, we visited Perth, Cairns and Sydney. We noticed that so many people were talking to us about the ways and means that we could emigrate to their beautiful country. Indeed, there had been a time when we'd considered this as an option when we applied for the Australian Police, but were unsuccessful. It seemed that the criteria at that time was service length specific and we had far more time in the Job than the authorities were seeking. It had been a fantastic place to live when I was in my late-twenties. Now a little older, I felt settled in my UK surroundings and appreciated just how idyllic my lifestyle and location was. I realised that I was actually very content to live in the UK, which is after all the middle of the world, yet Australia is remote. We felt that we'd struggle to improve on the life we already had.

Our final destination on this dream holiday was Hong Kong. On our last day we ventured to the Po Lin Buddha. At that time it was Asia's largest seated outdoor Buddha. At first glance it was concealed in the clouds, so a walk up the many steps was needed to properly view this impressive statue. Unfortunately the surrounding site was a rather tacky tourist retail area, with far too many souvenir shops and fast food outlets. There was even a cable car to take visitors around the site, if they were willing to pay the inflated prices.

With its heady scent of fragrant burning joysticks, we sought sanctuary from the hustle and bustle, retreating into the nearby Temple. Mystical lion statues, intricate wooden carvings and gold plated Buddha's filled this place of prayer, with offerings of fresh fruit being given to these objects of worship by many visitors. We were drawn to the rhythmical shaking sound of the Chinese fortune sticks. This is where we were instructed to get to our knees and pray whilst shaking the container of these numbered sticks. Holding the container at an angle, it was inevitable that one of the sticks would fall out. Matt went first and stick number ten fell to the ground. He took it to the monk who gave the reading,

' . . . *be satisfied with what you have. Don't waste your energy on hopeless dreams. What is in front of you is real and genuine . . . marriage is agreeable and a girl will be born . . .'*

When it was my turn, I dropped to my knees, closed my eyes tight and silently prayed harder than I'd ever done before.

"Dear Heavenly Father . . ." That opening in prayer has remained with me since my Mormon days.

"I love my darling Matt with all my heart and it would be the ultimate joy if we were blessed with a child. I try to picture what our son or daughter may look like, a little Mini-Me, Mini-Matt or a bit of us both! I stand in front of the mirror, pushing my stomach out and arching my back, visualising what I'd look like pregnant. It breaks my heart that I may not be able achieve this amazing goal, so for self preservation pray for your guidance on whether our plans for a family are achievable, Amen."

I shook the container vigorously, resounding in my head, *"give me guidance, give me guidance."*

Fortune Stick number seventy-three fell to the ground.

'The roar of thunder quickens the wheel of fortune. Circumstances have turned for the better. Such a big change in a single day. Like a somersault in front of heaven's gate. It is a successful year for you and your family. You are likely to come to fortune in spring. Marriage will be successful and you will give birth to a boy. There will be no problems for the ancestral graves.'

We walked away from the Temple with a spring in our steps, feeling positive for the future.

"That's it," I said.
"We are going to be successful with this IVF business. A boy and a girl? Well, it's our fate, we're going to have twins!"

Chapter Thirteen

LUCKY, LUCKY, LUCKY!

IT FELT WARM AND snuggly with the three of us tucked all cosy beneath the duvet. Matt was snoring, as usual, although he was insistent that this was in fact a contented purr. I was cuddled up to little Jack. Although it was starting to get light, it was still far too early to start the day. Jack was wriggling around and was becoming agitated. In order to investigate the possible cause of his restlessness, I patted his bottom through the outside of his baby grow, feeling that his nappy was now warm and heavy.

I scooped him up in my arms and climbed out of the bed, walking through to the bedroom next door, where I was all prepared. The baby changing mat was laid out on the bed, packet of nappies, wet wipes and powder, all to hand. Once the change was done, I carried him on my left hip, going downstairs to get the pre-prepared bottle out of the fridge. I gave it a quick blast in the microwave, had a little suck on the teat to check the temperature, then handed it to Jack. Without prompting, he began sucking on the bottle, more as comfort, than for the contents, as I could hear him sucking up air. We got back into bed and I placed Jack between Matt and I. I just needed a little more sleep, so squeezed my eyes shut, instructing Jack to do the same,

"Night-Nights now my little darling . . . close your eyes and have a little sleep, there's a good boy."

It felt like I'd been asleep for ages, but it was probably more like twenty minutes later when I stirred to the weird feeling of having my eye lashes delicately stroked. Jack's tiny little fingers were softly running their way along the tops of my lashes and as I slowly opened my eyes. I saw Jack looking inquisitively at my face, whilst his bottle was hanging out of his mouth as he chewed on the teat. Matt turned to face us both and together we snuggled around little Jack.

"He is such a dear little boy," said Matt. *"We could be laying here in a couple of years time, just like this, with our very own son or daughter,"* he continued.
"We get up now Auntie Me-Me?" questioned Jack in his baby language.

"Yes my little sweetheart," I assured, *"Your mummy will be coming to collect you very soon."*

We were under no illusions that the IVF journey was going to be a long and challenging one. However, on reflection, I don't think there was anywhere near enough preparation we could have done to cushion ourselves from the full impact it was going to have on both our life and future relationship. For some time now I'd been back and forth to my GP, checking the latest policies regarding IVF funding by the Primary Care Trust (PCT) in our area. I read more newspaper articles talking of a Post Code Lottery and that some PCT areas allowed couples three funded attempts, as per the recommendations made by the Human Fertilisation and Embryology Authority, yet some areas made no such funding. My local area maintained that just one attempt would be funded to women thirty-six and over. No matter how many times I wrote letters, appealing for special consideration to be given to allow me my one funded attempt whilst I was a little younger, my appeals were turned down.

Once I reached my thirty-sixth birthday, I revisited my GP. She made the appropriate referral and after about a month, we were given an appointment to see the fertility doctor at our local hospital. We followed the directions to his clinic, which rather insensitively was in the Maternity Department. And so, as Matt and I sat in the unfamiliar surroundings of this designated waiting area, situated by the main entrance doors, pregnant women would pass by as the baby and toddlers TV information channel was set on a repeat cycle.

We'd been waiting for five or ten minutes when Simon, our work colleague walked in with his pregnant wife. We exchanged brief pleasantries and they continued on their way. A few minutes later we were called in to see Dr Patel. He explained that at this time, we were likely to meet the criteria for PCT funding for one IVF cycle. However, we would need to have various tests carried out to establish whether we were actually able to commence with IVF treatment.

The tests were intrusive to say the least. They involved us giving various samples or blood, semen and smears to check for all sorts of sexually transmitted diseases including HIV. There was to be a check on sperm quality and whether my body produced sufficient follicle stimulating hormone (FSH) which in turn would assess my likely egg quality. We were warned that there were times when these tests indicated the couples were not suitable for IVF treatment, so we should take one step at a time. Dr Patel instructed us to see his secretary to collect all the necessary forms and directions.

Miss Snelling was a willowy looking lady in her late-forties. She had greying, long, mousy brown hair and wore drab attire. A pair of bifocals propped themselves half way down her nose. Her office was next door to Dr Patel's consultation room. She seemed a little unsure what forms she should be giving us. She was nervously fiddling with the corners of the various bits of paper, deciding which ones we should and should not have.

"Ummm, this is for your, err, the FSH test. I think it needs to be done on day four of your cycle at Pathology. Matt, this is the form you will need to do for your sperm count. I'll have to check where that needs to be done. These other forms will need to go with you to our GUM clinic in the north wing of the hospital. You can get those tests out of the way today as it's an open clinic."

On Miss Snelling's instructions we headed straight for the Genito-Urinary Medicines Clinic. We gave our names to the receptionist, along with the forms we'd just been given. We then sat in the waiting room, flicking through out of date magazines, where this time, Phil and Fern were entertaining us on day-time telly. It's was called the GUM Clinic, but it might as well have been named the STD Testing Clinic. It's one of those places that you do not want to bump into someone you know.

"Oh, 'Ello, I haven't seen you for a bit. How are you?" said the blonde female stranger sat the other side of the coffee table.

"Fine thanks," said Matt hesitantly, putting on an animated smile, whilst sinking a little lower into his chair.

"Who's that?" I whispered.

"Oh my God, that's the last person I wanted to see in here," shuddered Matt.

"I know her as a customer at work. She is such a gossip. I expect she'll thrive on telling people she's seen me in here. People will probably assume that one of us has been over the side and caught something."

"Michelle, can we see you for a moment," called the receptionist. She handed me our various forms.

"I've checked with our manager and we are not supposed to do these tests in our clinic for the purpose you need them. It's is not within our funding criteria. I can only suggest that you return to Miss Snelling and explain this to her," she advised.

The humiliation of not only being seen in the GUM clinic by someone known to us, but then getting evicted from that clinic, in the knowledge that we didn't actually need to be there in the first place. It was unbelievable! My annoyance was hard to conceal as we marched back to Miss Snelling's office and explained that we'd been refused testing. All nervy and dithery, I thought Miss Snelling was about to burst into tears, so I backed off with my initial confrontational tone. She left her office briefly, then returned with the information that we should see the nurse at our local doctors surgery to have the tests done. This seemed to make far more sense and we left the hospital feeling like there had been some progress that day, if only a little.

When it came to Matt's intimate sample being given, we had to go to another hospital and I waited in the car whilst he did the deed.

"Job done. How embarrassing! I had go into one of the toilet cubicles to knock one out. I did what they said and kept the container under my armpit to keep it warm. I then had to go to the sliding window and ring the bell for the nurse to come and take the container from me. They've checked under the microscope. They call them swimmers. They say they look strong and healthy."

We had no reason to doubt that Matt would pass with flying colours. He was fit and healthy, having a good diet from all my home cooking. He'd been following the recommendations in my fertility guide book, having his three Brazil nuts a day with his cereal. This guide book had become something of a Bible to me of late. I'd repeatedly read through it, making sure I hadn't missed or forgotten anything important. I took the very best multi-vitamin tablets, started taking folic acid and ate a diet that included oily fish and lots of organic fruit and vegetables. I personally thought the guidance of consuming only glass bottled mineral water was over the top, but had stopped drinking tea, coffee and fizzy drinks. I opted for herbal teas of various flavours and skimmed milk. I'd long since given up the Marlborough Lights and chose not to participate in the passive smoking, ensuring that I avoided being around smokers. I loved my red wine, but was not tempted by even the smallest of tipples. This project was far too important to contaminate my precious body with alcohol.

With my regular hounding of Miss Snelling, questioning whether test results were back, I was relieved to finally be told that all was in order, funding agreed and a referral made to place us on an IVF programme. I was overjoyed to get the letter from the private fertility clinic inviting us to an appointment within the next few weeks. I'd already saved up some leave days from work, opting to forgo some of my holiday period so I had enough allocated time off to make clinic appointments.

We took the day off from work and excitedly made our way to the clinic, which was nearly a two hour journey from home. A contemporary modern looking building in a residential back road was our destination. As we walked into the building and up the stairs towards the clinic, we were confronted by a mass of baby photographs proudly framed on the walls. On closer inspection, twins were scattered within this mix of little faces. The reception desk and signing in book was directly opposite the entrance door, with a healthy number of Thank you cards on view in the staff office, directly behind the friendly looking receptionist.

"Get yourselves a drink from the machine and take a seat. Someone will be with you shortly," she said.

It was one of those posh drinks machines, where you select the hot drink you want from the extensive range of sachets, poke one into a pocket on the machine and the rest is automatically done. Mine was a mint tea whilst Matt chose cappuccino. Even the basket of individually packaged biscuits was the more extravagant variety. They had those crumbly honey soaked oat cookies and melt in your mouth shortbreads. By now, my body was a temple, so I declined these treats, opting for a piece of fruit at times when a tea-time snack was required.

I looked around at the two other couples in this bright airy waiting room. They looked of similar age to us. They appeared comfortable in this environment and I sensed this was not their first visit. The man of one couple was called away and it was glaringly obvious what he was about to do. He departed with a handful of bulky newspapers. I questioned whether he had an adult magazine or two concealed somewhere within that bundle, to perhaps assist with the task in hand.

"Matt and Michelle, would you like to come through," said the kindly looking lady dressed in a white button up tunic. She introduced herself as Rebecca and explained that she would be our IVF consultant throughout the forthcoming process. She confirmed that they had received confirmation that this first cycle of IVF was to be funded by our PCT. Funding included all the medication, blood tests, scans, embryo retrieval, transfer and follow up consultation after treatment. We were told that the funding also included the freezing of any spare embryos for up to five years.

I'd already done my own research into what IVF was about, which made it a little easier to take in what Rebecca was saying about the process. I recall having a couple of lessons in the science lab at school, where we dissected a flower when being taught about reproduction. On another occasion just the girls were taken into a separate room to talk about periods and menstrual cycles. That's when we were given a booklet sponsored by Tampax, to answer any other embarrassing questions. However, apart from that, I'd never had reason to research the ins and outs of reproduction until this whole IVF business came to light.

I learnt that females are born with around two million eggs, then every month about twenty begin to develop in the plum sized ovaries. But there's only enough hormone to mature one egg to develop in the follicle sac. The nineteen or so shrivel away, and with a surge of Luteinising Hormone, this causes the release of the egg from the follicle. It can then begin its journey down the fallopian tube, where it may meet Sammy Sperm en route. The egg has started its journey, but the ruptured follicle still has a job, because it turns into a small cyst which produces Progesterone. That's the stuff that causes the womb lining to thicken, so that a fertilized embryo has somewhere to bed down and turns off other hormones.

So for me, a mature egg was never going to be able to make a journey down the tubes to meet Sammy, because there were no tubes. There were also no test tubes, but there were Petri dishes. With In-Vero Fertilization, mature eggs are collected and get introduced to Sammy in the dish. If all goes well, then Sammy gets it together with Egg and fertilization takes place. In some cases, fertilization doesn't happen because of the quality of the egg or sperm. Once fertilization has taken place, the embryo starts to develop cell division and after two days are ready to be placed in the womb. That's when it's hoped that the embryo will continue to develop and bed itself in the womb. If all goes well, then two weeks later a pregnancy can be confirmed.

Rebecca advised us about projected success rates. Based on our age and the fact we'd be undertaking a fresh cycle of IVF, there was a thirty percent success rate of pregnancy. In comparison with frozen cycles, where the frozen embryos are defrosted and used, the success rate was around twenty-five percent. She went on to say that because two embryos are transferred at a time, there was a possibility of multiple births and a natural risk attached to that. We were somewhat bombarded with various facts and figures, but the words which resounded in my head were the positive ones of "success" and "possibility of twins."

During that first visit they did a pelvic scan. I had to sit on a blue paper sheet, lay back on the couch, shift my bottom to the edge, spread my legs slightly apart and pop my ankles onto the stirrups in front of it. With Matt stood next to me, this was a position I was to adopt on many future occasions. A lubricated cold probe was gently pushed into my vagina and a TV monitor in front of my chair displayed a blurred black and white image, which changed its distorted smudge with every movement of the probe. The consultant pointed out various blobs on the screen, explaining that one bit was my womb and that the stumps of my fallopian tubes were visible. She warned that ectopic pregnancy could not be ruled out just because I didn't have operating tubes. She said it had been known for an embryo to embed itself in these stumps and if that happened the pregnancy could not continue. She did however assure that at present, all appeared in order and we were advised we would be given another appointment date at a set day of my menstrual cycle.

We left the clinic on that beautiful sunny April afternoon, with a new found positive outlook to this whole baby making project. The timing seemed perfect, with success rates apparently being greater in the Spring, as it's a time for growth and renewal. It felt like it was a case of *when* I get pregnant, rather than *if*. It was briefly explained to us that the facts and figures were in relation to pregnancy, rather than *live births*, not forgetting that miscarriage can happen.

Just to be pregnant at some point in my life was really important to me. There had been various medical questionnaires that I'd completed over the years. They asked if I'd ever been pregnant and I had to answer *No*. I'd spent all those years having those inconvenient periods and monthly stomach pains . . . and for what? To be pregnant at some point in my life was all about actually using my female operating tools. In a diary entry I wrote the following,

I liken myself to a Ferrari! A fine specimen of a motor car that is sitting on the production line. It's complete and ready to be driven to its full potential, longing for the key to be put into the ignition and to hear that engine roar for the first time. That for me would be getting pregnant. Now, I may never be able to actually get to release the handbrake and press down on the accelerator, which would be the birth . . . but just to hear the engine roar, knowing that something has functioned within this beauty of a machine would in itself be success.

I was in the office at work a few days later, tapping out a crime report relating to a domestic I'd been to an hour earlier. My ear piece was concealed under my hair, irritating the inside of my ear lob, handcuffs digging into my ribs, my bulky body armour unzipped to allow a bit of air to dry out my sweaty shirt; just a normal day. PC Simon Coe came in and sat at the computer monitor next to me.

"You should be taking it easy . . . in your condition," he said with a cheeky smile and a wink.

I was rather confused because I currently had no *condition* and had not even started the IVF treatment at that stage. I then had a flash back to when Matt and I had been spotted by him in the Maternity Department of our local hospital. He clearly thought I was pregnant!

"Umm, it's business as usual for me Simon," I said, trying to buy some time to think up what to say, to save him from feeling uncomfortable or embarrassed.

"You should be on light duties by now. When's it due?" he asked enthusiastically.

"Oh Simon, how funny, I'm not pregnant! The day we saw you at the hospital, we were seeing the IVF doctor. It's okay, we're cool about it all."

I'm not sure how poor Simon could have responded to my answer, and thankfully he wasn't given the opportunity. A call came out on the radio and he rushed away to attend a road traffic accident.

With another visit to the fertility clinic, they confirmed blood tests showed I was ready to start the treatment. They advised that medication had to be tailor made to suit each individual, so placed an order of the concoctions they felt I would need. They gave me a little green rucksack type bag, with a handful of tablet boxes and needles. There were clear instructions of how I should self medicate and inject. The quantities and medication would differ depending on what day of the cycle I was on. To start with I needed to begin by injecting Buserelin, which is part of the down regulating process. This was the medication that was going to put me into a type of menopausal state, so that the clinic could then take control of my menstrual cycle.

A few days later a package arrived for me at home. I opened the bulky polystyrene box to find ice packs chilling numerous vials. A multitude of medication was within, with directions of which ones needed to be refrigerated. Yet more syringes filled the box, along with tablets, suppositories and a pregnancy testing kit. Seeing this testing kit made it feel like there was a very real possibility that a baby really could happen for us.

My hands were shaking as I drew up the fluid into the needle from the little glass bottle. I flicked the syringe as I'd been told, then grabbed a fatty handful at the top of my right thigh. I could see all the puckered little fatty cellulite lumps on the surface of my skin as I wiped the piece of antiseptic wipe against it. I prodded the skin surface, trying to prepare myself to sink the needle in. As I hit the spot, breaking the skin, pushing the contents into my thigh, I decided that it wasn't that bad after all. The needle was thin and sharp, I had plenty of thigh padding, so there was just a bit of discomfort, rather than pain. However, with the Buserilin came the headaches. Previously, I'd rarely experienced headaches, apart from when I'd had a bit too much to drink the night before. These Buserilin headaches were different. They lasted most of the day and no matter how much I rubbed on my temples, they wouldn't let up. It was at this point that I started scanning through the various chat room forums on the internet, reading about other people going through the same thing as me. It seemed these Buserelin headaches were not uncommon.

Back at the clinic, a blood test confirmed that the Buserelin had been doing its job. They could now take control of my cycle and move onto the next stage of stimulating the ovaries to produce multiple follicles. The consultant explained that they would need to monitor progress and possibly adjust my dose of medication, depending on how my body reacted. The monitoring continued with visits back and forth to the clinic for tests. There were so many visits that I suggested to Matt that I go alone on some of these occasions.

It was during one of my lone visits that I adopted the position, had the probe inserted and watched the blobs on the TV monitor. The consultant pointed out what looked like a bubble,

"Oh dear," she said, letting out a big sigh.

"I was hoping not to see this. The scan shows that you have a cyst. It's nothing dangerous, just a pocket of fluid, but we need to carry out a cyst aspiration, so that we can drain the fluid. If we don't do this, the medication can't work properly."

She said that I'd need to be sedated for the procedure, would need to be escorted home and be unable to drive for twenty-four hours. They called Matt. He dropped everything to travel over to meet me. By the time he arrived I was starting to come round from the procedure and had been given the obligatory cup of tea and biscuit. I'm sure this must have been a very difficult time for Matt. He must have felt so helpless, having to see me go through the stresses of procedures and medication, yet having little involvement at this stage of the process himself. Thankfully, the cyst aspiration had been successful and I could continue with my daily injections, which by this time had given me a cluster of bruises on my thigh. One of the nurses suggested that I might like to try injecting in my stomach rather than the leg. For me, this became the preferred option. I'd need only to pull my top up slightly, pinch just below my belly button and go for that spot, which didn't bruise.

After I'd started my period, the Buserelin injections continued. I now also started to inject a follicle stimulator, where I'd have to wind the pen type needle holder, to adjust the amount of fluid it was to release, dependant on what the clinic were advising me to take. This was the stuff that was going to stimulate my follicles, so that rather than just one maturing, many more would. It was at that stage that things could get a bit risky. If the hormones were not quite right, over stimulation could occur, resulting in too many follicles maturing. If that was to happen then a condition called Ovarian Hyper-Stimulation Syndrome could occur, which could cause severe pain, breathing problems, vomiting and faintness. In some cases it could even result in a heart attack, thrombosis or a stroke.

Another scan showed an image of something looking like a dried poppy pod. From this, the nurse was able to confirm that I was responding well to the treatment and had twenty-one follicles developing. I was concerned to hear I had so many, because I'd heard ten to twenty follicles was expected. The nurse assured me that all was fine and I should continue with the treatment.

As the days went on, my lower abdomen felt heavy and tender. It felt uncomfortable to wear jeans or clothing tight around my waist. Travelling over speed humps was not desirable because the movement caused discomfort, as if I had a full bladder. With this feeling, the continued injections and the visits to the clinic, IVF was in the forefront of my thoughts all of the time. It could be no other way. I found myself noticing pregnant women wherever I looked. They were everywhere and I suspect I may have spotted some that didn't even know they were pregnant themselves! When I looked in clothes shops, I was drawn to the baby clothing section. I'd handle the pretty little lacy dresses, mittens and booties. I'd picture what my own child might look like in them and feel so very tempted to buy some of the outfits, because they looked so beautiful.

Having confirmation that my follicles were now of a desirable size, I had a date set for egg retrieval, which was a Wednesday. I asked my duties office for the time off work for this important date, but was advised that I'd need authorisation from a Sergeant before this could be allowed. Either way, I was going to attend the clinic, with or without permission. It was somewhat frustrating to go through this process, but at that time my employers had no policies in place to cover this issue. Thankfully, the Sergeant gave his blessing without hesitation and I was granted annual leave. By now, I was already working out what my due date could be and what months I would be on maternity leave. I was also considering if I would return to work three months after the birth or if Matt would be the one to go part-time to cover the child care.

On that Monday evening I was alone as Matt was on a late shift. I kept checking the clock, which seemed to be moving around slower than ever. 10.30pm was the deadline and I didn't want to get the medication prepared too early before that time. I was worried that it wouldn't work properly if it was taken out of the fridge too soon. At 10.25pm, I took out the two small boxes from the fridge. My hands were shaking as I snapped the glass top of the vial. I was so worried that I was going to spill the contents and mess up the whole procedure at this crucial stage. I followed the instructions, drawing up the liquid from this vial, which then had to go into another one and get mixed. I then had to inject myself with this preparation of Human Chorionic Gonadotrophin, which triggered the final maturation of my follicles for ovulation, so that my eggs could be collected thirty-six hours later.

We were up very early on that Wednesday morning, only too aware that it was such an important day for both of us. Throughout the journey to the clinic, I was rubbing gently on my heavy stomach in circular movements, the type that pregnant women do. The baby photos seemed more prominent than ever as we walked up those steps to the clinic, picturing that our baby would be joining the hall of fame very soon. Matt and I kissed, bidding one another luck as we were ushered in different directions. I was taken downstairs to get undressed and put on a blue hospital gown, walking into the theatre wearing my blue paper slippers and hair net. With the instructions to count down from ten, I made it to eight before I was sedated.

It was at this time Matt would have been providing his sperm specimen. To this day, he has declined to go into detail with me, but I can only imagine that it must have been one of the most bizarre acts he and any other man has been asked to perform. He would have been alone in a room with a chair, with the blue paper towel laid over it. A plastic sample container would have been in one hand whilst the other hand was busy perform a sexual act. I guess he would have had to think erotic sexual thoughts in order to do so. The pressure was on because this ejaculation needed to be the best ever from a set of platinum bollocks. With all this in mind, the stark facts could not be overshadowed. This act was all about making a baby and needed to provide the best sperm ever in order to do so. Failure was not be an option for Matt, knowing that I had been through weeks of intensive treatment and that I was on the operating table at that very time when the wanking process was in full speed.

I woke feeling a little disorientated and groggy, but was elated to hear that twenty eggs had been retrieved and were now with the washed sperm awaiting the fertilization process. We were advised that we would need to call the clinic the following afternoon, when they would be able to give us an update. They had checked my womb lining to see that it was thickening as they had wanted, so it seemed the anal suppositories I'd been inserting had been doing their job. For now, there was nothing more we could do but wait.

The following day, we were told that a spectacular number of eggs had fertilised. We were thrilled with this result! There were some woman who were lucky to have had just one fertilized egg. Matt got on the phone to one of his friends, who was keen for an update.

"Kev, as expected, I have super sperm, because we've got fourteen fertilized eggs. We're back at the clinic tomorrow for two to be transferred to Michelle. I knew we could do it! This big old house of ours is gonna be full of kids in a few years time!"

On the Friday, we turned up at the clinic very excited. We both had to wear the blue paper slippers as we went into the operating theatre. I laid out on the bench with legs apart, TV monitor in front and Matt holding my hand. There was no pain involved in this procedure. A catheter was inserted into my vagina. We watched on the monitor as two white dots illuminated on the screen and the catheter was then removed. Rebecca explained that the dots were the fluid containing the microscopic embryos. We were given a black and white scan picture of our dots, which we proudly admired, just as any other couple would their three month baby scan photos. With a grin from ear to ear, Matt pointed to the dots on our scan picture,

"That's little Meghan and that one is baby Max," he gushed.

We felt so blessed that we had achieved this crucial point, because we'd heard that other couples failed to get to this stage in their treatment. We'd also heard of the success stories from friends,

"Michelle, I've got a friend who did IVF and had twins on their first attempt."

I'm not sure if these friends were all talking about the same couple, but it seemed the talk was only of success stories about IVF. The newspaper headlines continued to report on the progress with IVF treatment and Hello magazine followed the story of yet another celebrity in their forties who'd had their own IVF baby.

For the next few days, rest and relaxation was paramount to me. This was the time that the embryos would be developing to attach themselves to my thickened womb lining. I followed the instruction of being optimistic. I kept my thoughts and was lounging around as much as possible. Being lazy was not in my nature, but I knew it was so important to do as little as possible, so that my body could concentrate its energy on baby making.

When I was on my own, I'd close my eyes, put hands on my stomach, take a deep breath through my nose and say to myself,

"My embryos are healthy and growing, my womb lining is thick. This is working and I will find I am pregnant."

The timing could not have been better to coincide with some physiotherapy I needed on my knee, with a pre-booked stay at the police rehab centre arranged. So there I was, a couple of days after the embryo transfer, heading for a ten day stay at this luxury retreat. I'd remembered it as a great place during my last visit, where I had of course found a husband. However, I was rather limited with activities during this second stay. The IVF consultant had advised that I should try to maintain a stable body temperature, which meant no swimming or sauna's. Even a soak in the bath was out of the question. There could be no tipsy joviality in the cheap on-site bar, nor could there be a sweaty work out in the gym. Instead my days were spent mainly in solitude. I'd go for walks alone, or sit in my room drinking herbal tea and of all things, knitting! Over the following week, I was busy doing rows of plain and pearl to create a healthy number of squares. My Nan had got me into this temporary hobby, which she too participated in. these knitted squares were gathered up by her social club members, who turned them into blankets to be shipped off to disaster zones by some charitable organisation.

I was bored though, very bored. I found myself wishing the time away to the date when I could find out if the IVF had worked. I bought one of those magazines for pregnant and new mothers. It had a double page spread in it, showing the development of a foetus. I pictured what my baby, or even babies, may look like in a couple of months time. I saw an advert for one of those 3D scans and decided that I would of course be needing to have one of those.

The problem with this two week wait was that I didn't want to wait for the result. I wanted to find out before the two weeks were up. I'd read that doing a pregnancy test too soon could give a false positive result because of the IVF drugs in the system. However, there were times when a correct reading could show up in the second week of the wait. The temptation was too great and I found myself in a chemist, selecting a twin pack of pregnancy testing kits. For some reason, I felt like I was doing something very naughty, like buying a huge chocolate bar that I was going to scoff myself without anyone else knowing. The test needed to be done first thing in the morning, so I thought of nothing else as I tossed and turned, trying to get off to sleep. I woke at 5am and wondered if that would count as my first wee of the day. I decided to go for it and did a wee on the stick, hoping for the little blue cross to appear. I checked after a minute and a single horizontal line was faintly appearing. I thought that if I wait a little longer then the vertical line would also show through, but it didn't. I consoled myself that it was still early days and even if I was pregnant, my body would not yet have produced enough of the pregnancy hormone to be detected. I continued the rest of the day knitting and drinking herbal tea.

By the morning of day eleven, I was starting to feel different. I felt more tired and tearful and had a heavy feeling in my stomach. Could this be the feeling of pregnancy? I decided to use my last spare pregnancy kit and as I waited for the result, thoughts flashed through my head. I was thinking about how I'd announce my pregnancy to Matt and whether I should tell him now or when he was expecting the result on day fourteen. However, with the display of the bold horizontal line, I was again filled with disappointment, but reassured myself that I did have another three days to go until day fourteen.

During a trip to the toilet later that same day, I detected what looked like blood on the tissue, but I thought I may be mistaken. However, there was no mistake a little later, when I began to bleed heavily as I started my period. I was devastated and poured out my sorrow to Matt who was on the other end of the phone. He called the clinic who advised that sometimes bleeding could occur when the embryo is bedding down in the womb lining. I was still to do the test on day fourteen as planned.

As far as I was concerned, the journey on this occasion was over. Matt sounded frustrated, if not annoyed with me. I'd gone against the guidance of the clinic and done the test early. It felt as if he was suggesting that my early testing had brought about the failure of the IVF treatment. This was of course not the case, but just like me, he too was flooded with disappointment at this devastating result by day fourteen.

I returned home early from the police rehab centre. There seemed no point being there anymore and I now needed to be doing things to take my mind off my failure. Matt and I got our bikes out and cycled out to meet my parents who had already been updated with the news. I knew they too were disappointed, but did their best to hide this. After initially expressing their condolences, they helpfully carried on as normal, as if nothing tragic had just happened. For me, it felt good to finally exert some physical energy after weeks of enforced resting.

I allowed myself a long awaited glass of wine, which I have to say did not taste as good as I'd been expecting, probably because I'd lost a taste for it after the prolonged abstinence. I cried. We both did, as it felt like a bereavement, yet there had been no perished soul. The loss turned into anger, when we'd see so many undeserving parents who seemed to be able to pop babies out left right and centre. They were the ones with an ulterior motive. For them, having babies allowed them to be entitled to social housing, child benefit payments and lots more freebees for The State, so they could continue with their alcohol and cigarette habits. Why did God choose to allow the bad ones to be gifted with children and not the good ones? It all seemed so unfair.

It was around this time that people I knew were showing off their babies. The other mothers would hover around them, cooing at its little whimpers and cries, begging to have a hold of the tiny bundle. I did my best to pretend I was interested, but the fact is that I was not. I didn't want to have a hold or a cuddle of someone else's child. I wanted my own and the fact that anyone else had a baby and I didn't, all seemed very unfair.

It must have been a very difficult time for Matt because few people would enquire how he was. He hadn't been the one having to put his body through the physical demands of the treatment. To others, the impact of the emotional demands he'd suffered remained undetected. He must have been screaming inside, feeling so powerless, seeing me go through the treatment and the aftermath of that.

It's in his nature to be the strong powerful all action hero and protector. However, in this situation, Matt must have felt like he'd been chained up and powerless to protect the one he loved the most in the world. Matt did give me strength though. He reminded me that he loved me no matter what. If we were not destined to have children, then he would not stop loving me because of that. We still had another ten frozen embryos and with that an opportunity of further attempts. He assured me,

"I never fail at anything. We can do this. We can make this happen, Lucky!"

At times, Matt would refer to me as *Lucky* as a nickname. This was a sarcastic reference to the fact that there had been many occasions in my life, where luck had not always been on my side. I think this side of me goes back as far as my police cadet days, when I was given the Endeavour Award. This was to credit my character, that sometimes my goals may be a struggle for me, when others may find them a walk in the park. With lots of effort and determination I do get there in the end. It was clear that the baby making thing was not going to come easy, but I was sure to put every effort into it.

We returned to the clinic some weeks later. They explained that the majority of couples are not successful during their first round of IVF and suggested I give my body a break of a couple of months before we start with the next round.

CHAPTER FOURTEEN

LET ME LEAVE ME FOR A WHILE

"*DING, DING, ROUND TWO*," I said as we arrived on that crisp autumn morning at the clinic. I'd adopted a fighting spirit, ready to win this round, because this time it was costing us money. The first IVF attempt had been funded, but unlike other areas, we had to pay for further attempts. I'd been saving for this for some time now, so financially, we were prepared. Physically, I was rested and repaired from the last treatment. Emotionally we were stronger and more positive than ever.

Rebecca explained the pros and cons of pursuing IVF with our stored frozen embryos. Success rates were a lower twenty-five percent, rather than thirty-percent on a fresh cycle. But, the benefits were that I didn't have to put my body through the process of producing lots of mature eggs again. There was also a significant difference in the cost of the treatment.

We signed all the necessary forms and I paid the bill in advance for the treatment. The spending did not stop there, because a couple of days later I got the call from the drugs providers. They wanting my bank card details for the order which ran into hundreds of pounds. A few days after that I got one of the polystyrene boxes delivered to the door. Once again, it was filled with syringes, tablets, suppositories and vials that had to be stored in the fridge.

I picked up where I left off with those Buserelin injections. Yet again the headaches were with me, but that was fine. My body was prepared with the hormones to be accept the embryos and once the scans confirmed my womb lining was thick enough, the embryos were defrosted. Five needed to be defrosted from our stash, as they were not all expected to survive a thaw. Two of the highest graded embryos were selected. After several weeks of repeat visits to the clinic for blood tests and scans, the microscopic dots were once again placed in my womb. The two week wait commenced, but this time I went to work during this period.

I'd secured myself a Monday to Friday office hours position, so it was a lot easier on my body with the set routine. Whilst at work, I had other things to think about, like crime fighting and investigations, so had no choice but to deviate my thoughts away from the subject of IVF.

By day fourteen I had no period and had done no sneaky early pregnancy tests. But, having had failure the first time round, I was a little more realistic about the possible outcome on this occasion. Matt was at home when I did that first wee in the morning. I've no doubt that at the moment of testing, he had everything crossed, willing for me to return to the bedroom to announce I was pregnant. But I couldn't do that, because the result was once again negative. I wiped the tears from my cheeks and took a deep breath. I was intent on being strong because I didn't want Matt to see me as a crumbling wreck. I came back into the bedroom and didn't need to say anything because he just knew. But I couldn't stop my flooding tears. I went to say something, then let out an almighty sob of despair as he wrapped his strong protective arms around me, assuring me that he loved me unconditionally, no matter what.

There was little time to stop and begin dissecting the events or to discuss our disappointment. I don't think we really needed to because we'd been there and done on the last occasion. I had to be in the office for 9am, so just had to get on with it. I turned up as usual, got on with my work and disappeared every now and then to have a quick cry in the toilet cubicle, to let off some of the emotional grief. The only person I could really talk to about my turmoil was to Matt, because he understood. He felt it too.

One of my dearest friends was pregnant at the time with her first child. It didn't seem right to burden her with tails of my devastation, when she was so excited about the forthcoming arrival of her child. When talking to friends and associates, I tried to portray a less emotional attitude about the IVF failings because this was my coping mechanism. I'd say things like,

"It's not the end of the world. At least I can now have a drink over the Christmas period and won't look fat for our wedding anniversary photos!"

If I'd been telling them the truth, I'd have said something like,

"I'm completely devastated. I feel like such a failure. I feel so terribly guilty that it's all my fault that Matt and I are in this

situation in the first place. I would be quite happy to never drink again if children depended on it and I would have loved to look pregnant in my photos."

Such a statement would of course have come with a whole lot of sobbing from me. I've no doubt it would have left others feeling uncomfortable talking about their own pregnancies and children around me.

Matt was in the habit of clearing his mobile phone of messages sent and received. He also did that with the computer, clearing it of history details after he used it. I felt assured that he didn't do this to hide some devious activity. It's more likely he simply did this to keep neatness and order. Knowing he did this, I left a somewhat cryptic message for him by searching sentences, which in turn left a history, which he'd see if he checked. My searches went something like,

I AM SO TERRIBLY SORRY
I FEEL LIKE I HAVE FAILED YOU
I BROUGHT THIS PROBLEM INTO OUR RELATIONSHIP
AND I HATE MYSELF FOR HURTING YOU WITH MY
PROBLEM
IT'S ALL MY FAULT, NOT YOURS.

A few days later I got confirmation that Matt had been oh so predictable. He had indeed gone through the computer history and seen my message. Sitting beside our big fluffy teddy bear was a letter. This letter was written in a style as if the teddy had written it!

Hello Michelle, I bet you didn't know that teddy bears could write! Matt has been chatting with me and asked if I would

pass on his feelings to you. We thought it would be better to write something, because you'd probably try to interrupt him if he was to say it. He says that sometimes spoken word can be taken for granted.

He is so proud of you, with the dedication and commitment you have given, trying to extend the numbers to your lovely home. You are so special to him and he loves you very much. In fact, hard to believe possible, but he loves you more with each moment that passes by!

He finds it hard seeing you go through torment and tears with what you're both going through. He knows that if you both stick together you'll probably conquer all, no matter what you are up against!

Since he met you his life has changed beyond comprehension. He didn't think he could love someone so much. He's so content and happy.

He's told me he has transferred money into your account. This should cover most of the funds for your next cycle. He knows too well that you both deserve this and you're not going to let this beat you. The opportunity is too important to let money be the deciding factor in calling it a day. In the same breath though, he worries so much that this whole thing, like the medication etc, is hurting you and making you more upset. That's his only worry.

All I ask, knowing full well what you mean to him, is that you forget this mindset that you have, thinking that it is you that has brought this unfortunate situation into your lives. Don't take it upon yourself to think this is a failure on either of your parts. Let's face it, when have either of you been given anything on a plate that's worth fighting for?

Every time you suggest it's your fault, STOP, because that makes him feel excluded from you and so hurt. You have jointly been dealt with this hand, so are both in it together.

He has asked me to reassure you that these thoughts you have are never in his thoughts, far from them. You are to carry on and do what you feel is right at the time. Let's face it girl, neither of you are poor and you are better off than many.

The long and short of it is that he wants you to continue with what you both do, which is fight for what you want and don't let anything stand in your way. He was somewhat concerned when he found some words on the computer. He thinks you may have left these words for him. He thought perhaps you were working far too hard and going nuts. The words you left caused him some mixed emotions!

It hurts him to think you feel alone in all of this. It's not YOU, ME or I anymore girl. It's US.

I know that by the time you read this letter, he will be at work. Although he is not with you tonight, there is not a single one hundredth of a second when you are not in his thoughts. Michelle, you are a special girl in his eyes. Don't forget it! xxx

I burst into tears on reading Matt's letter. They were tears of relief that his love for me had not faltered and that he didn't resent me for my perceived failings. However, with regards to the financing of the IVF treatment, I remained insistent that I should fund this in its entirety. After all, I had the money saved up, got a slightly greater income than him and had no plans to spend the saved money on other things. At that time no money had reached my account and I suggested to Matt that he cancel any money transfers, because for now I was content to fund the third IVF treatment as I had done the previous one.

On reflection, this financial decision caused me issues which I recognised further down the line. My funding of the treatment and Matt's acceptance to allow me to pay, served as an indirect way to validate my feelings, that the fertility issues we faced were my fault and therefore my responsibility. With this self induced blame came a burden of guilt that I chose to carry.

Before embarking on round three, Matt and I went away for one of our beloved city breaks. This time we chose Amsterdam. Being a small city, apart from some limited use of the tram, we did our sightseeing mainly on foot. We briefly walked through the red light district, but we were more interested in the clogs, tulips, canal trip and the Van Gogh museum. There was no allure to the many coffee shops dotted around the city. In fact, I could hardly tolerate walking past them as the pungent smell of skunk was sickening. However, for some unknown reason we found ourselves slightly off the beaten track in a little circular traffic free zone. There in front of us was a building with a big bold name above it of MAXIMUS. Was it fate that we'd found ourselves at this destination? Perhaps we were being given a sign to say IVF was going to work and that our son Maximus would be born!

A week after returning from this trip, we were back at the fertility clinic for an appointment to arrange our third

IVF attempt. Rebecca explained that it would be best to use all five remaining embryos for this round. They could then select the best from those that survived the thaw. She recommended Blastocyst as the success rates could be higher. She explained that the embryos were placed in a special culture to develop for five days, rather than the usual two. They are then transferred to the womb. We took her advice and agreed to the Blastocyst procedure. We paid the usual fee for a frozen cycle of IVF, along with an additional £500 for the special culture that our embryos would be placed in.

Once again there was the arrival of the expensive pharmaceutical products, bag full of syringes and the little yellow needle bin. I started the Buserelin injections and made numerous visits back and forth to the clinic for various blood tests and scans. Yet another cyst was detected to attempt to hinder the process. However, I'd become so accustomed to the discomfort and intrusion of this whole process and agreed to have the cyst aspiration without sedation. That way, I didn't have the twenty-four hour driving ban, nor did I require an escort home. Although a little uncomfortable, the cyst aspiration was more than achievable without the sedation and I was able to leave the clinic a short time after the process to continue with the drugs I was taking.

It was around this time that Matt and I visited a dear friend who had recently given birth. Both her and her husband beamed with elation, showing off their new addition to the family.

"Michelle, the feeling you get when you are holding your own baby is the best in the world! The immense love you feel is indescribable! You'll see, when you have one of your own."

I had to take a deep breath before I gave any response, because I knew that I may never feel that love that people had told me about. I may never hear someone call me "Mummy."

"Well, we'll have to wait and see," I said. *"There is only a twenty-five percent chance of success in each round of IVF and we might not get lucky."*

My friends husband somewhat reprimanded me for my apparent negativity,

"You can't think like that. You'll have your own one day, you'll see," he said.

Matt and I had talked many a time of how many IVF attempts we should make. We knew that not only was there the physical and emotional strain, but also the financial burden. How can we put a price on a child? was one side of the argument, yet do you continue gambling on IVF until you are crippled up with debt and still have nothing to show for it? Did it matter if we had to re-mortgage or perhaps sell up and live in a tiny rented home, if we had our very own child to show for it at the end?

For me, one of the things about having a child was about having eternal life. The birth of my own son or daughter would serve as an extension of myself and they would become far more important to me than my own life. My love for them would commit me to give my own life for them if I had to. It was about securing a forever bond between my beloved Matt and I, that no one could ever take away.

The clinic confirmed once again that my body was ready for the transfer process to take place. They removed the five remaining embryos to thaw and explained that they would prepare the Blastocyst culture for them to go into. However, we got a call earlier than expected, calling us into the clinic for an early transfer. We were told that only two embryos had survived and that transferring them straight to my womb rather than to the special culture was preferred. The fact is that if the embryos had perished whilst in the culture before reaching the Blastocyst stage, then there would never have been any transfer. This in itself would have been hard to accept, taking into account that I'd spent weeks taking drugs to prepare my body for that process.

Once again, Matt was by my side as the embryos were placed in my womb. We were given the scan picture of our dots and started the two week wait. The Human Fertilization and Embryology Authority (who we had to pay a fee of over £100 for each IVF attempt) recommended three IVF attempts, so there was a lot of hope attached to this round. We really felt we'd done all we could. Success seemed closer than ever.

But that's just it. It wasn't successful. Another negative pregnancy test was the result at the end of our two week wait. This time the result felt more final.

"We've given it a hundred percent Michelle. Perhaps we shouldn't mess around with nature anymore and just accept that we're not going to have our own children," appealed Matt.

"But we haven't given it a hundred percent. We've only given it eighty," I sobbed.

My reasoning behind this eighty percent figure was that the first round of IVF had offered us a thirty percent success rate and the others twenty-five, as frozen embryos were used.

Another round of IVF would cost in excess of five grand. Although this was achievable for us to fund without running into debt, Matt was going to struggle to see me go for through the harsh treatment of producing a whole batch of fresh eggs and having to start back at square one.

I was now a year older and statistically, with that, came falling success rates. I could have coped with taking all the medication again and was willing to put my body through the harsh process. However, this wasn't about me, this was about us. I had to accept that it was too much for Matt to cope with emotionally. He didn't want to feel he was in that straight jacket, powerless as he witnessed me going through turmoil, unable to protect me from the pain and heartache of yet another IVF attempt.

I started to research other avenues, looking into IVF abroad and even adoption. A Chinese baby looked appealing, but stories on the internet suggested that the pursuit of such a child would take in excess of two years with a fee of over twenty grand attached.

We chose to explore the option closer to home, making contact with our local Children's Services Department. One of their representatives visited us at home and invited us on an adoption course. It ran for a period of around eight weeks and consisted of evening and weekend sessions with other couples all keen to adopt.

We went along to the sessions for about five weeks, but after that time, we felt sure that adoption was not for us. It clearly takes very special people to go down the adoption route. We felt that we'd always have someone else's child and in effect be like glorified babysitters throughout its childhood. Don't forget that many of these children were going to have extended family and grandparents. They'd still want to be involved in their life. Because of that, the occasional visit would need to be arranged for that to happen. We were advised of the memory boxes that were put together by the birth parents. If the child had questions about their parents later on in life, they could refer to the memory box, as and when it seemed like the right time to do so. There were of course those children who have been sexually abused and would never be having contact with their birth parents or extended family again. Those children may want to give us a *Special Kiss*, because that's a behaviour they'd previously been taught. We were asked to think about how we'd deal with such events and behaviours.

Matt and I were only too aware that there were some poor little souls that had a terrible start in life. Those that got passed around to various family members and foster parents before they were finally put for adoption. Many of those children would be pretty screwed up by the time the adoption process took place and that could be difficult to deal with. There are those that were born to parents who had learning disabilities and may therefore be born with disabilities themselves. Those children who had been created by violent evil parents, who may themselves have such a nature in their genes. Having attended the classes, we decided that adoption was not for us.

At that at time I still hadn't completely ruled out another round of IVF. However, as time went on and those IVF drugs got out of my system, the strong desires to have a child started to subside. I began to feel rather conned by the whole IVF business. After all, it was a private business, based on making a profit out of other peoples hopes and dreams. We were sold those twenty-five and thirty percent success rates. But, let's get real with it. In essence, we are buying into seventy to seventy-five percent failure. Don't forget that those statistics were based on pregnancy rates. There were many women who succeed in getting pregnant, but went on to miscarry. I knew a positive mindset was advisable when going into the IVF process, but I really don't think the sales pitch pushed the fact enough, that failure was the most likely outcome. I saw all those baby pictures up on the wall as we went into the clinic. How about a wall full of childless couples who tried and failed? Now that would be bad for business!

CHAPTER FIFTEEN

LET IT SHINE

"*Oh, he is lovely, I want him Michelle, I want him!*" whispered Matt excitedly.

The adorable little boy was running around the room, playing with his brother and sister. He was the dark haired one, whilst the others were blondies. He had big dark eyes and a button of a nose. The lady scooped him up in her arms and snuggled him inside her jacket.

"We call him Chocolate, but that's not his Pedigree name. I have all the certificates that come with him," explained the breeder.

We hadn't specifically planned to go out and get ourselves a pet dog that day, but during a slightly drunken trawl on the internet the night before, we'd spotted an advert regarding a Chihuahua puppy for sale. We got drawn into this particular advert as coincidently, the breeder was from our village. We had no reason to shy away from our curiosity because the puppy was just around the corner from us. We needed to convince the breeder that we'd make good parents to Chocolate, then we headed to the pet shop to buy a bed, carry container, lead, food, toys and all those other pet essentials. Once we had collected up the goodies, we returned later that day to collect our little boy. We named him Maximus.

Being such a small breed, this tiny bundle of fur was so delicate and vulnerable. We cuddled up around him, spoke softly to reassure him that he was safe and cared for. But poor little Maximus had to be left all alone for long periods whilst we were at work. We hated doing that to him. We spoke with the breeder about our concerns and she offered a solution,

"My granddaughter was supposed to have the bitch of the litter, but I've ended up with a vet bill for one of my other dogs, so need to sell the bitch to pay that bill. She's yours if you want her," she said.

So, within a few months of the arrival of Maximus, we welcomed his sister Minimus into our family. Our dear little Minnie and Max were perfect together and brought us so much happiness. I'd had pets before, but Minnie and Max were different. They meant so much more to us. They'd come at a time when we were searching to love and nurture a little being. The bonus for us was that we had two!

I still had the niggling thought in my mind, that maybe I should have another go of IVF, so as to never look back with regret. But, as time went on, Matt did not encourage such thoughts and I began to really embrace the idea that I was to remain childless. I started to recognise that children were not the be all and end all in my life. There were so many bonuses to being without them. Ok, I was never going to experience that *immense love for your own child* that people had told me about. But, how can you miss something you've never had? I wasn't going to be without love, because I had the continued love from Matt. I also had the love I gave and received from the two little dogs. I heard many people say,

"Well, they're only dogs,"

To us, Minnie and Max were very dear. There was no 'only' about it.

There was no definitive date, nor any specific conversation that cemented the decision, but as time went on, we both came to the conclusion that we had ended our IVF journey and would not be re-visiting that path again. It got easier with time, because for me, time ran out as I became too old to realistically consider IVF. Yes, I heard that there were women in their forties that had children. Lots of them. But for those that found success with IVF, they may have had to use donor eggs, which I didn't want to do. Unlike me, other older women may have been able to conceive naturally. I personally felt that with regards to childbirth, the door had closed and was locked for good.

There were times when people said to me,
"No children then? I suppose it's because you've chosen to be a career woman rather than a mother."

I'd come out with some light hearted excuse, when I really wanted to say something like,

"There was a time when I would have loved to have been a mother and given my dear husband a son or daughter, but nature has decided that I shall be barren."

Someone once said to me,

"Michelle, you were never that bothered about having children really, were you."

I did reply to that, quite simply, by saying,

"To embark on IVF you have to be a hundred and fifty percent bothered about having children."

I found there were times when friends had become pregnant, they'd be reluctant to break their good news to me, feeling awkward that they were boasting a dream I could never have.

Thankfully, I didn't look back with regret, because that was the hand I'd been dealt and I had to go on. Rather than mope around feeling depressed about something I could never have, I took the attitude that I loved the fact that I could be selfish. I could spend my money on myself rather than on child care fees and kids clothing. I had time to go to the gym and I didn't have a saggy stomach or stretch marks. I didn't suffer from a lack of sleep because I have had to get up for night feeds nor did I have to deal with childhood sickness bugs and head lice. I didn't have constant back ache from lugging a son or daughter round on my left hip, nor were my clothes soiled with baby sick or caked on food.

However, I retained a sense of guilt for failing to give Matt the child I knew he really wanted. That was just something I had to carry and a feeling I had to suppress.

We had been putting aside money for an IVF round, but now that we'd decided that wasn't to be, we were intent of having some fun with the savings. We planned another fabulous five week holiday, revisiting Australia to catch up with Sadie, Cole and Tommy. A stopped off to explore the cities of Beijing and Tokyo was planned either side. We had an early morning start to the trip, so dropped Minnie and Max off with our friends the night before. It was strange being without them, because this was the first time we'd not been as a family since they'd arrived with us.

Our travels started in Beijing, where we got a taxi from the airport to our hotel. We were amazed that our twenty five minute taxi ride had cost less than a tenner. That became our preferred form of transport, hoping in a cab to get to the various markets and sites. We hired a taxi for the whole day for eighty pounds, taking us to The Great Wall, Summer Palace and Birds Nest at the Olympic site. We were intrigued when some of the Oriental visitors were waving their cameras at us and we assumed they wanted us to take their picture. However, that wasn't the case at all. They must have thought we looked like one of their favourite Hollywood film stars and wanted their photos taken with us!

We searched for somewhere nice to eat, but this proved difficult, with many of the menus consisting of bull frogs, sheep tongue, fish heads and other culinary delights. The Food Market offered other tantalising treats of grilled star fish, caterpillars, sea horses and fried beetles. I'd always been game on to try anything once, but Matt was not so keen, so we settled for noodles and rice.

The following morning we were back at Tian'amen Square. It looked completely different from the previous day. It was now packed with hordes of Chinese visitors, all uniformly dressed in red baseball caps. They were queuing around the Memorial Hall to pay their respects to the preserved body of Chairman Mao who died in 1976. We were keen to enter The Hall, which was only open during the morning. So, we were rather concerned to see the lengthy queue, which would have left us in line for at least a couple of hours, and perhaps out of time to get in. We towered above the others and were quickly spotted and approached by a suited man. He offered to speak with his corrupt security friends and get us to the front of the line. A deal was struck and ten pounds poorer, we were entering the hall.

The others in line were hardly able to contain their excited emotions, trying desperately to push forward, then be pulled back by the guards. People were buying Chrysanthemums to then place beside the many other flowers at the seated memorial statue just inside the main building. We were convinced that the security guards would routinely clear these flowers away to resell them on again. As we were ushered into the resting area, we saw the body of Chairman Mao in a glass top coffin with two guards beside him. During that five second glimpse, I saw what resembled a wax work figure. Within moments it was all over and we were ushered out of the hall and into a small gift shop.

The Forbidden City formed part of the tourist route, for us and thousands of others that day. Once inside, we found it crammed full of those Chinese visitors. I witnessed what I can only describe as a frenzy, with the crowds all trying desperately to get a glimpse of the inside of the various rooms. Visitors were not permitted to enter, only look from the outside. There was a lot of pushing and shoving from all. We reaped the benefits of our height and stature, being able to glance over the top of heads and get a good view, even from a distance.

As a little girl I'd been a Blue Peter fan. The presenter was Sarah Green and she was my role model. I remembered how they'd followed the beginnings of a Chinese Panda and filmed the Zoo where it had been born. A visit to the Beijing Zoo was therefore a once in a lifetime experience that I could not miss out on. Matt and I were surprised that the Zoo entry fee was so cheap, but it was once inside that we discovered why. So little money appeared to have been spent on staffing, surroundings and care for the animals. We found the experience rather disturbing. The Brown Bear enclosure displayed a huge sign, NO FEEDING, yet there was no supervision to stop the cruel visitors pouring down their fizzy drinks and cakes, so as to get those bears onto their back legs. This was done to provide a photo opportunity and some cheap entertainment. The Rhino paced back and forth on dry soil without any signs of water. The animal appeared to be in a state of madness. This mirrored the surroundings for most of the other creatures, apart from the Pandas. They were getting the five star treatment in comparison to their neighbours as they were clearly a good money spinner, with the well stocked gift shop dedicated mainly to them.

Sadie and Cole joined us for our Sydney leg of the trip. This being our second visit to the city in recent years, we travelled around confidently, knowing where we wanted to be and how to get there. A boat trip took us to the beautiful town of Manley, where we walked to Cabbage Tree Bay and the beautiful Shelley Beach. The sun was blazing and the blue waters sparkled.

"Now I could live in a place like this," said a contented Matt, as we lunched out at Le Kiosk, sipping on a very cold glass of Pinot Grigio.

Our crammed itinerary included our attendance at The Sydney Opera House to see a world class conductor present a symphony, with a finale of Land and Hope and Glory.

"Wow, this is amazing. That music always reminds me of my Nan," said an awe inspired Matt.

His fear of heights had Matt declining to partake in a climb up the Harbour Bridge with me, so instead he opted for a flight experience in a simulator, entering the replica of a cock pit, where he became the pilot of a Boeing 737, taking him to Hong Kong and back within an hour. I personally found this attraction rather boring from where I was sitting, in the rear of the mock plane. Although rather expensive, we felt it was worth the attempt to help Matt with his fear of flying.

Our timing in Sydney was perfect as the film AUSTRALIA was about to hit the box office. We were in the city for the arrival of the star studded cast attending the premier night. We were snapping away on the camera as the likes of Hugh Jackman, Nicole Kidman and Brian Brown stepped out onto the red carpet. Although it rained, we didn't care because we were there in the thick of it all, seeing these A—listers that we'd only ever seen on the big screen or in Hello Magazine.

On our arrival in Perth, we hired a car. We picked up Tommy and started our five day trip North to Monkey Mia. After a few hours of driving we arrived at our first remote location, The Pinnacles in Namburg National Park. It amounted to thousands of limestone pillars protruding from the golden sand dunes. It was hot and dry with an eerie silence, giving a feeling of a huge cemetery full of tomb stones of various heights. We continued on as we had a lot of driving to do in a day, stopping at the blue waters and rather windy jetty at Jurien Bay, then onwards along the North West Coastal Highway to Geraldton. On our arrival in this little town we saw the corn silos and Port Moore Lighthouse dominating the skyline. We stayed in a motel beside the beach and continued on towards Northampton the next morning.

It was en route that we stumbled upon a little tearoom called Oakabella Homestead. We drove up the dusty driveway, reaching a farmhouse and wondered if anyone was in. We parked up and sauntered around the desolate site, which claimed to be the most haunted place in Western Australia. A short lady in her fifties appeared from a doorway, startling us at first with her wild eyes and unstable expression. She spoke with a strange Canadian/Irish/Australian accent and fed us with her huge scones and tea. I was a little sceptical about consuming these, fearing that she might be poisoning us, with plans to chop us up and bury us on her farm, to join all the ghosts she spoke so vividly about.

The map up to Monkey Mia basically showed a long road North, then a left turn. It's just before that left turn that we came across the Billabong Tavern. With a sign of life in such a remote area, we decided to stop for a drink. We were greeted by an old, miserable looking, unfriendly chap. I parted with the money for three coffees, for him to point to the hot water urn and instant coffee powder tin, directing us to make our own drinks.

With a left turn and about twenty minutes later we arrived at Hamlin Pool. This was an historic telegraph station, where a short walk took us to the Stomatolites. They looked a bit like huge mossy people just below the water. A drive further on had us at Shell Beach, which looked white. On closer inspection we found it was made up of tiny sharp cockle shells, making sunbathing on such a beach impossible. Unless of course, one had a fetish for laying on a bed of nails.

Our final destination that day was Denham, arriving late in the afternoon. Although the travel brochures suggested it to be a lively resort, that did not quite appear to be the case. It had a couple of pubs, off licence, grocery shop, garage, a restaurant and little else. It was the Old Pearler Restaurant that enticed us in with its unique selling point. It was the only restaurant in the world to be built predominantly of seashells and is the was the most westerly restaurant in Australia. It was a BYO, so we stopped off at the bottle shop for the wine to go with our seafood platter, just in time to watch the orange and red glow of the sun setting.

We'd travelled all that way, which was some five hundred miles to get to Monkey Mia. This resort was about a an half hour drive from Denham and consisted of nothing much more than holiday chalets, and visits from Dolphins for feeding three times a day. There was some temporary excitement when a tannoy announcement ushered visitors to the waterside. We subserviently went to the set location, discarded our flip flops and dipped our feet into the water. We were instructed by staff that we were not allowed to wade in further than our ankles.

I can't have been pushing my chest out enough, Matt not smiling broadly nor Tommy waving his arm sufficiently, for us to be amongst the special chosen few who were allowed to feed the dolphins. They were the ones who were permitted to get their knees wet and take fish from a bucket to give to the tame creatures. The feeding frenzy was over as quickly as it had started and we were left with nothing much more to do than walk along the beach and sunbathe.

It was during our drive South back to Perth that we came across the most dramatic scenery around the area of Kalbarri. A half hour drive along the bumpy unmade road led us to Natures Window. This was an orange coloured rock with enough room for a couple of people to perch inside for a great photo opportunity, framing a spectacular back drop of wilderness. The poor hire car bumped its way back to the tarmac and onto the small town of Kalbarri.

A place called Finlay's had come highly recommended for its barbeque menu, so that's where we dined that evening. It had a unique charm, with tired discoloured plastic patio table and chairs, a roll of toilet paper taking the place of napkins and the water served in disposable plastic cups, the type that become misshaped or split with the slightest over zealous squeeze. Grungy rock music played as the bearded biker guy cooked up our steaks and served our mixed salad from a pre-mixed bucket of the stuff by his side. The food was good value and I had no complaints about its flavour or quantity, but sensed Matt was not impressed as he liked the finer things in life and to him this was roughing it.

The following morning we went to a grassy area beside the seafront where a sign had advertised Pelican feeding at

8.45am. A small group gathered for this free show and sure enough a flock of around ten Pelicans arrived on cue. This time, I was the special chosen one and was handed a slimy dead fish by the guide. This was eagerly snapped up by the bird, who managed to chomp off a bit of skin from my hand with his meal. Being the brave soldier that I was, I had no hospital treatment, not that it was offered. Instead, I dabbed my wound with a little tissue paper until the bleeding stopped.

We continued down South to the various rocky coastal beauty spots of Red Bluff, Castle Cove and Natures Bridge, before we got to The Pink Lake. True to the guide book, it was indeed pink, if not a little lilac in colour. I was told the colour was caused by the Beta Carotene in the soil beneath the water.

Our five day excursion had taken us over thirteen thousand miles of road and given us a taster of remoteness of a previously unknown entity. Being reunited with civilisation in Perth was welcomed by us all, which I embraced with a visit by me to the beauty salon to get my gel nails redone. The rest of our time in Perth was spent visiting a few old haunts like The Blue Duck Café in Cottesloe, Burswood Casino and a winery crawl around the area of the Swan Valley.

Our final travel destination of Japan was something of a wild card as I'd planned to book us for a stopover in India. It seems fate was kind to us. Our choice not to go there meant we dodged the horrific tourist killings in Mumbai. When we heard the breaking news of the attacks, we knew how easily that could have been us as the victims of that terrible blood bath.

It was evident that my hours of trawling the internet, looking for a good deal, had paid off. We were staying in a fabulous top rated hotel overlooking Rainbow Bridge and a mock Statue of Liberty, in the trendy area of Tokyo's Odaiba. Whilst sitting in a café watching the world go by, we noticed a trendy looking Japanese lady in her twenties, pushing a cute little Dachshund puppy in a pushchair. This looked just like the sort of pushchair that you'd expect to see a child seated in. On closer inspection I saw it was actually designed specifically with dogs in mind.

We couldn't believe our eyes when we then saw a middle aged lady, walking by with two little long haired Chihuahua's trotting behind her. One was clothed in a pair of jeans and black leather look jacket. The other wore a mini-skirt and pink jumper with a heavily diamond encrusted collar.

"Oh, I miss my babies," gasped Matt. *"I can't wait to see my Minnie and Max,"* he sighed.

We quickly jumped up from our seats and followed the trendy little dogs. We wanted to watch them for just a little longer, thinking about our own little furry babies. And that's when we realised they were all around us. Lots of little dogs and not a naked one in sight!

The little creatures followed their keeper into a pet shop. The pet shops I had previously been accustomed to, had that natural, almost farmyard straw smell. They usually had a healthy stock of dried pigs ears, ham bones and multi-coloured dog biscuits shaped in circles, squares and triangles in open boxes with scoops and bags beside them. There'd be a selection of dog collars and leads, offering a variety of sizes rather than styles. The bags of dried dog food would fill the shelves and pet clothing displayed would amount to a few tartan dog coats. At some of the better equipped stores, there would be a few T-shirts with PRINCESS or I'M CUTE on the back. The sales assistants would usually look a little ungroomed, as if she'd stepped out from a kennel.

Pet Paradise was nothing like that. We were greeted at the entrance by a sales assistant looking like she'd stepped off the catwalk. The store smelt of a seductive floral fragrance. The spot lighting illuminated a selection of sparkling pet jewellery and sunglasses behind the glass display cabinets. There were rows upon rows of dog jeans, skirts, dresses, jumpers and coats. Brands of Levi, Adidas and Nike were common place on these little outfits. We picked up the various items, picturing what our darling little Minnie and Max would look like in the clothing. We were working out what bags they'd like to be carried in and what pushchair they would love as their chariot. Needless to say that I made quite a few purchases.

I found Tokyo to be one of the most confusing and unique cities I have ever been to. All things considered, we managed to find our way around fairly well, but it was more about getting a feel for the place and people. Plastic display food was presented in the window of so many restaurants. There was no mistaking what the customer would be getting, as this was an exact replica of the meal. Vending machines were in abundance, with a drink or snack machine on just about every street. The buildings were modern and huge. A visit to the Municipal Government Building revealing glimpses of Mount Fuji on a clear day from the forty-fifth. Free hugs were being offered at Harajuka, by the wacky dressed youths at their Sunday gatherings.

The highlight of our visit was seeing those little clothed dogs. We were reminded just how much we adored our little babies and how much we'd missed them during our travels.

We were living the dream, doing all the things that so many people aspire to experience at some point in their lives. Some would have to wait until retirement, when health or finances may hinder their delayed travel plans. If we'd had children, we'd have been restricted from doing such amazing things. Money had been no object during our travel adventure. The way I saw it was, that we could have blown all those thousands of pounds on yet another failed IVF attempt and had nothing but heartache at the end of it.

Minnie and Max loved their new Pet Stroller, which looked just like a three wheeled baby buggy. I dressed them up in their designer outfits, although it was apparent that Max preferred to be naked. He loved being carried around in his animal print bag. Our friends were convinced that I was now completely Chihuahua bonkers!

We were now a proper family. Christmas and Birthday cards would be signed off,

'Love from Michelle, Matt, Minnie and Max xxxx,' and we'd proudly frame our family portraits of the four of us together. They had their own individual personalities and ways about them, that only their Mummy and Daddy would understand better than anyone else. Their picture became our computer and mobile phone screen saver. They had their own special

part on the sofa, where they'd sit on their very own hot water bottles for added comfort. A toy box would be filled with their favourite squeaking soft toys and chew sticks. We adored them and would proudly refer to them as "The kids." They were irreplaceable and filled the gap of being childless. Minnie and Max were a vital part in the healing process in accepting that we were never to have children of our own.

Chapter Sixteen

EVERYONE NEEDS A BOSOM
FOR A PILLOW

THERE IS NO DOUBT that our childless status and joint income gave Matt and I a degree of financial security, enabling us to make a few extravagant, indulgent purchases. Matt enjoyed his nice cars and sports motorbikes, getting all the matching accessories. I wasn't really one for the flash car and toys. I enjoyed the experiences, which is why I loved the great holidays, but I also loved the cosmetic enhancements. However, over the years I have learnt that if one is going to mess around with themselves, then there can be some pitfalls.

These days, I see so many young girls in their early twenties tottering around with their fake boobs. They will have been shown the most flattering before and after photographs, then manage to cut a good deal with a cosmetic surgery company, parting with three or four grand for their silicon enhancements. They can even pay by monthly instalments if required. I question whether these young women have really taken into account the additional expense they may be committing themselves to, in the years to come. They may close their ears to the fact that there is no denying gravity. As the years go by, even those voluptuous firm knockers will want to head south. The implants can begin to perish through age and they may need replacing.

It is also possible that the body will want to reject them, causing a build up of scar tissue around the implant to distort the shape and feel. Having been there and done it with the whole boob job thing, I would discourage any woman under thirty from breast surgery. There are some great chicken fillet enhancements and fabulous pretty padded bras available. These can serve a less endowed girl sufficiently to avoid the knife. However, I know what it feels like to have a mindset that you *need* those new boobs and will spend whatever it takes to get them.

I was twenty-nine when I got mine. I felt I needed them as my boobs had taken on that saggy deflated look. The quantity of skin on my chest did not match the amount of filling. The surgeon readily took my cash and did the operation within a week or so of me seeing him. The first three days after surgery were painful, but after that I was fine. Within two weeks, I was able to physically do most things. By that time they looked great, I loved the results and was more than comfortable at getting my tits out for the boys.

It was only a couple of years later that my right boob felt much harder than the left. It felt like I had a rock for an implant. The shape was not too bad, but the feeling between the two was distinctively different. As the years went on the shape of my breasts became more distorted. The only way to rectifying this look was through surgery, which I stalled off for as long as possible.

Some nine years later I had my second boob job. I had my smooth saline implants replaced with textured silicone gel, as per the recommendations of the highly regarded surgeon I had searched out. The surgery was nearly double what I'd paid the first time around. Everything costs money and I was having to pay for the implants to be taken out, scar tissue removed and new implants put in. All of that takes extra surgery time, so therefore an extra expense to me. I was advised that the surgery had been a success, all had gone to plan and I could expect to see a more final result in the following months.

As the months rolled by, the results were not so good. My previously rock hard right boob was now lovely and soft, but the left one had become rock like and distorted. The condition called Capsular Contracture had again developed. I'd already invested a lot of money in my chest, so was determined to see the job through, even if it was to cost a little more. The surgeon booked me in for corrective surgery and with another few thousand pounds spent, I had my left implant removed, the scar tissue cut away and the implant replaced. I'd hoped that was going to be the end of it, but there was more.

Three weeks after this third boob job, Matt and I went away for a city break to Las Vegas. We were having a lovely time and my boobs appeared to be looking great. I was hopeful that this time there would be no build up of unwanted scar tissue. I'd taken to massaging my boobs and would rub the area where the stitches had been to try to soften the unwanted lines. One morning during one of my rubbing sessions in our hotel room, the drama unfolded. As I ran my fingers along the bottom of my boobs by the crease, I could feel a warm wetness on the left side. I looked at my fingers and could see blood! I looked down to my boobs and was horrified to see the red fluid quite literally gushing from a hole in the stitch marks, under my left implant.

"*Matt, I'm okay, but there's a problem and I'm going to need some medical help,*" I said calmly, as I got up from bed and walked to the bathroom, leaving a trail of blood on the fluffy cream carpet as it squirted out from the incision. I got one of the white fluffy towels and pressed it hard against the hole. But, every time I lifted it away to see if the bleeding had stopped, it came gushing out as if a tap had been turned on. I knew I had to stay calm because I didn't want to go into shock.

"*Hello, reception? This is room 6117. We need some medical help. My wife is bleeding from the chest!*" said Matt with a distinct panic in his tone.

I had wrongly assumed that this big luxury Las Vegas hotel, which had a community of thousands of people, would have its own in-house medical team. I was therefore not expecting the arrival of two burly built security guards coming to our door, snapping on their blue rubber gloves, with one clasping what looked like a stun gun ready to zap Matt if needed. It seems that they were under the impression that they may have a domestic assault on their hands, where perhaps Matt had stabbed me in the chest with a knife. They softened their approach as I explained there appeared to be a complication with my recent cosmetic surgery. There was no ambulance and no medical team. Instead, we were given a card with details of several medical clinics which we could get to by taxi. The best they could offer was a priority position in the taxi queue outside the hotel. So, ten minutes later, I was walking through the hotel casino and reception area, trying my best to conceal my blood soaked towel wedged against my breast, under some baggy clothing.

Once we arrived at the clinic, they were not going to even speak with me about my problem until they had my credit card. Once payment was secured, I was seen and advised that a pocket of fluid had build up in my breast and it had been draining out through the hole. This fluid was discoloured by blood, so was therefore a red colour. I was relieved to hear that I was not going to bleeding to death, but was now prone to infection due to the open wound. I was bandaged up to compress the open area and advised to see my surgeon on my return to the UK a few days later. Within a few hours and a few hundred pounds in money lighter, we were out sightseeing once again.

A couple of days later, I was seen by the surgeon who put me on antibiotics for week. The hole was about a centimetre wide and would not close up. Instead it would ooze fluid and I'd have to place a sanitary towel under it to absorb the liquid. When I lifted my arms up, a farting noise would emanate from that area, as the hole sucked up air, then spat it out again with a dribble of fluid. I'd squeeze my boob in the morning, to drain off yet more fluid that had built up overnight. I was taking the antibiotics for weeks, having to tolerate that irritating side effect from long term used of such medication—Thrush! It took a further eight weeks for the hole to finally seal. I was just days away from the threat that if it was not to close, then that implant would have to be removed.

And as the months followed after the hole in the boob drama, the left breast became distorted and hard in places, just as before surgery. The implant had started to ripple under my skin and the best advice the surgeon could give me was to put on some weight, so that the fat could give some filling under my skin. I had to resign myself to the fact that the implants were not working for me and look at the other options.

I visited other surgeons. One suggested that he could remove the implant and replace it with another, but it was his preference to replace both at the same time. This made little sense to me as I had no problems with my right breast, interfering with it by having another operation could cause it problems. I went to another surgeon who suggested that I have both implants removed and to give my body a rest, before considering much smaller implants in the future.

"You might even decide that you like a small chest and choose not to have implants again," he said.

A year after the Las Vegas drama, I was back in hospital, having my 400cc of silicon and excess skin removed. My nipples were cut around and moved into a symmetrical position. I was stitched up with the circular, horizontal and vertical lines, scarring being left as a reminder of the history of my boobs, to fade with time. My chest had cost me thousands and we had a great time together, the boobs and me. But, they have been the full circle and some sixteen thousand pounds later were back to where they were eleven years earlier.

I've tried the Intense Pulse Light treatment, attempting to have unwanted leg hair removed with a laser by a specialist.

It was usual to have around six courses of this treatment for the desired results. However, I was only able to suffer one, having been badly burnt by the procedure, left with burns and blisters and pigmentation damage for over two years. I went on to have successful IPL treatment in other areas of my body, but the messing around with yourself business has a risk attached with most procedures. It's worth taking this into account before diving in to have things done.

I became a lover of Botox. I still am! The downside being that it is expensive, costing around three £300 to get the wrinkles around the eyes, forehead and frown softened. I've found that the results look great for the first three months, but treatment twice a year appears sufficient. I've found that it really does get rid of those lines in the way that those expensive creams never did. My Botox usually takes no longer than half an hour to be done. The results are not instant as it can take about five to seven days to set in.

"Why do you have this fear of aging?" I'd be asked. *"You look lovely. You don't need Botox,"* say many of my friends.

I try explaining that I have no self image issues. In fact, I continue to be very happy with my appearance, but I do all these things because they are available to me and because I can afford to do it. I'll never need to save my money for a child's future university fees.

"It's like my hobby, I look good because I have these treatments" I say. *"I love trying all these procedures. If they are good enough for the celebs, then they are good enough for me!"*

Botox aside, I do recognise that I naturally have good clear skin. I am aware of the damage sun can do and continue to use a high SPF sun cream.

Derma fillers are another of my secret pleasures. I find the injections uncomfortable, rather than painful. Lip fillers work really well for me. They cost around the same price as Botox, but are great value, in the way that they give instant results and in my experience last for about a year.

As for piercing, well, I've already told you about a few of those. Personally, I'd advise against a tongue piercing. I found it hard to resist that temptation of playing around with that piece of metal permanently in my mouth, which resulted in a few chips to my teeth. It had to go, as did the nose piercing. That little bit of metal struggled to stay in my nose and didn't actually look that pretty. It may have done if I had one of those cute little pixy noses, but I don't.

I'm like a kid in a sweet shop when it comes to a beauty salon, although I have to say that I'm not great at maintaining the treatments. I enjoy getting my nails painted or the gel extensions with glitter tips applied. But, you'll find me a few days later, doing the gardening without gloves, digging out the moss and weeds from the paving with my bare hands.

The lash extensions are so relaxing to have applied. With the instructions that I need to lay back and close my eyes for an hour, I find myself drifting off to sleep and waking to find I have the most amazing Bambi, Porn Star length lashes to last me a couple of weeks. However, I get into the bad habit of picking at the glue of the lashes and end up making my lids a little bald in patches.

Decorative toenail coverings are good fun and last for well over a month. Then of course there is my hair. I like to appear well groomed and insist on getting my hair cut and coloured every six to eight weeks. I enjoy all these self indulgences and hope to continue with them for many years to come. I wouldn't rule out a face lift or whatever else takes my fancy, but I'm a few years off that yet.

I've continued to maintain the semi-permanent eyeliner tattooing. It's well worth the pain for the results, which last about a two years. I have a few body tattoos too. However, I advise anyone to be really happy with your design before getting anything permanent. The colourful swallow seemed so trendy twenty years ago, but doesn't look quite so artistic now, being slapped on my back in its more faded form.

I had the blonde hair extensions in Australia all those years ago, hoped I'd learnt my lesson, but still went on to do it all over again with the long brown locks. Once again, they lasted me no more than three months before I could tolerate them no longer, when I resorted to ripping each tangled strand out of my hair. I have since opted for the multi-coloured wigs as my preference, to accompany one of my many fancy dress costumes. Oh, how I love the fancy dress theme! At a party I can be anyone I want to be, whether its Cat Woman, Wonder Woman, a pirate, trucker girl, Lady Christmas, Lady Ga-Ga, a fantasy cop, Tarzan's Jane or even Ethel aged nine.

CHAPTER SEVENTEEN

I WISH NOTHING BUT THE BEST FOR YOU

No matter how much I tried, I could never stop showing off a huge cheesy grin. It was one of those smile where my upper lip tucked itself in to stick to the top of my gums, revealing most of my top teeth and a big line of pink gumminess above it. Matt and I would do that thing, where we'd be out shopping and suggest go off our separate ways, then meet back at a certain time and place around an hour later. That's the unavoidable grin I would be wearing, as we spotted one another from a distance on the approach to meeting up again. He would do it too. He'd say he was grinning at the fact that my grin looked so ridiculous, but I know it's because he felt it too. He felt so happy that he was with me and we loved one another so much.

We'd been through so many experiences together, both happy and sad, but we'd got through the other side. We made a good partnership. We were a dab hand at joint projects because we knew how one another worked, our fields of expertise and what the other was thinking.

We planned for the future. We predicted we'd be getting a pension after thirty years service, so by the time we reached our mid-fifties, we would both be on retirement pensions and have a regular income from that. We talked of getting a large camper van and travelling around Europe to escape our British climate during the winter months. We would of course be going on regular cruises and exploring the world.

We'd open a little restaurant offering a limited but tasty menu. I'd be in the kitchen cooking up the delights, whilst Matt charmed the customers, taking the food orders and encouraging the purchase of the profit making drinks. Having no off-spring to visit us in our care homes in the future, we'd flee to Thailand where we'd live like Royalty and employ Phee-phee and Phu-phu to look after us in our later years.

We didn't have it all worked out, but we did feel that no matter what, it would all work out well. We felt we didn't need children because we had each other and that was the most important thing of all.

However, there were cracks in this picture of domestic bliss. They had been there for so long, that I think we had leant to live with them. I continued to carry an inner guilt, feeling that it was because of me we had been unable to have children. To make myself feel better about my perceived failings, I'd be very giving with my money, but subconsciously feel resentful that Matt was readily accepting of such generosity. On reflection, I feel I am a such a strong character that I offered him little choice other than to accept my gratuities without protest.

Somewhere along the line intimacy left our relationship and we stopped fancying one another. We continued our mutual adoration, which threw our feelings into confusion. We discussed our intimacy issues from time to time and resolved to jointly combat the problem. However, we'd become more like brother and sister than husband and wife. Once it had reached that stage there was no going back. Our relationship had taken on a different form and it was irreversible. That said, we remained content in our day to day routine, happy with our work and home life. We owned our own houses. Matt remained financially tied to his own property with the commitment to house his beloved Nan. So, my property was our home and we were quite settled there.

There have been some good times and some turbulent ones within my own family. There have been times when my family has offered me so much love and support, yet others when that love has come with conditions. Through the good times and bad, I retain a feeling that I belong somewhere, that there were a group of people care about me and will continue to do so throughout my life. Being part of a family is of importance to me, because it's a feeling of belonging that I like to have. Matt has a small family and has no siblings. For much of his childhood his single parented mother lived with her mother, which in turn meant he spent most of his younger years being brought up by his grandmother. He adored Nan and ensured that she continued to live in the home she'd spent half her life in, by buying it so she could remain there. Although there were some distant family members, they did not form part of his unit, which amounted to Matt, Nan and Mum.

Nan was well into her nineties when she suffered a short illness which resulted in her going into hospital, never to return home. Within the space of just four months, Matt experienced his grandmother's sudden ill health and subsequent death, having to support his mother through the stress, emptying and selling the home Nan had lived in for fifty years, arranging her funeral single handed and buying another property. Throughout all of this pressure, he continued to be the all action hero at work. I admire him for his determination and outstanding achievements at such a difficult time. The sense of loss for Matt was immense, because for him, he had lost something huge. He had lost fifty percent of his family and he was devastated.

For me, this served as a reminder of that guilt I carried. The guilt that I could never provide Matt with a family. I would never be able to give him a son or daughter that would always be his, no matter what. This was a guilt that was not going to go away. However, the timing seemed to offer a possible solution for me, a way to try to release that guilt, before it was too late. We had to face the issue that due to the lack of intimacy, our relationship was not what it should be.

Matt was still in his early forties, remaining as charming and good looking as ever. He was still at a time in his life, where if he had the opportunity to do so, he could meet a woman of child bearing age who could give him what I could not. She'd be able to give him a family and in turn release me from my guilt. We'd both be winners. We'd both be losers. In my experience, loss can be hard, but one does get over it eventually, because you have to. I am only too aware of the emotions that follow a separation or an ending of a relationship, but the emotional hurt does heal and it's possible to move on.

I struggled to shrug off this idea as a solution. Matt did nothing himself to make me feel guilty for being unable to give him a family. I did that all by myself. But the more I thought about it, the more I yearned to finally be free of my guilt. I carried it for far too long and as the years ticked by, it got worse, not better. Although I felt calm that the door had finally closed for me in terms of having a child, the door for Matt was still ajar. It could be wide open again, if it was pushed in the right direction. I would have looked back with so much regret if I'd done nothing to push that door open for him.

And so, through the many tears and emotional turmoil that followed, we concluded to part. We agreed that Matt would move to his own home and that we would remain the best of friends. After all, we remained the proud Mummy and Daddy of Minnie and Max and continued to share the responsibilities of caring for them.

I didn't want it any other way because I still adored Matt and simply wanted the very best for him. We had a mountain of photographs to record our fabulous experiences and I shall always treasure those memories which I shared with the most amazing person and great companion. Matt left a note for me, which read,

Michelle,

The word love is used to described many different feelings, acts and emotions. I have used the word many times to you! I want you to know that I love you with all my heart and despite what we are about to go through, I will continue to love you with all my heart for the rest of my life. I know we have decided to part full time company and remain friends, but I wanted you to know YOU WERE, ARE AND WILL ALWAYS BE THE ONE, but you know that. Thank you for wanting to carry on being my best friend. It means the world to me! I'm sorry I couldn't tick all the boxes of being a husband!

X Always X

There was a huge buzz and on the day we officially separated, which I take to be the day that he got the keys to his new home. There was a great sense of wellbeing and enthusiasm, with the masses celebrating, clinking the champagne glasses, waving flags and proclaiming that the bride and groom did indeed make a wonderful couple. This was the day that Kate and Wills got married and the day we parted. Nothing felt negative about this day, because it was the start of a new adventure for the two of us. We'd had a successful marriage and were now in a successful separation. I believe that people are good for one another at said periods of their lives, but as individuals they may change and not be so good for each other forever. We were good for one another for those years we were together and we'd continue to be good as friends once apart.

As I went through our possessions, separating Matt's personal belongings from my own, I came across the memory album from my first wedding and read my writings of my aspirations from nearly twenty years earlier. I considered whether I'd achieved my goals. I lived in a big house, it wasn't in North London, but it was in the area of my choice. I didn't own pine furniture as it was rather outdated by now, but I was very content with my Balinese pieces. I didn't shop in Marks and Spencer's for my weekly groceries because Sainsbury's was local and I'd since become a Lidl fan. I had a wardrobe of lovely inexpensive clothing and had been on the most fabulous holidays. I was content that I had indeed met the challenge I set myself all that time ago, but it really wouldn't have made any difference to my happiness if I hadn't. After all, they were rather shallow goals set at that time.

I hadn't been able to meet the dream of having lots of children, all sat around a table with sticky back plastic and glitter, making some ornament out of a used margarine container and a washing up liquid bottle. However, I felt I had now given Matt the opportunity to pursue this dream, but perhaps I got it all wrong. By now, I'd started writing this book and in effect it served as a therapy and a tool for me to get to know myself. Matt sent me a text,

'You must make it clear in the book, because it is important. We had a true bond and we were only ever going to be parents together because of the love we had! I could never consider children without you. Hopefully the penny will finally drop about how much it all meant to me. Without you in the equation children will not feature. I sometimes think you didn't take on board my words. Suggesting I could go on to have children is to me as painful as not being able to! I don't want to talk about this again.'

I am under no illusions that if Matt and I had been successful in our pursuit to have children, then we would have remained together, with or without a satisfying sexual relationship. However, we were not meant to be and I am of the belief that there is little point in dwelling on the past in a negative light. We must embrace the experience and be open to new opportunities that form from the end of a chapter in one's life.

Chapter Eighteen

READY FOR LOVE

THE BOOK WRITING HAD already commenced before Matt and I parted. I must confess that I had little idea of what the ending of my book would be at the time I started it. I'd never expected this one, that's for sure! It had been quite a journey, but I was feeling calm and content about my future.

I was now middle aged, single and childless, yet happy with my status. I had a lovely group of friends and never felt lonely or bored. I made a few changes to my home to make it feel like my own again and resigned myself to the fact that marriage and I did not mix. I'd reached that age when I still tried to cling on to what was going on with chart music, but struggled to know most of the latest pop groups and found myself preferring those 80's and 90's classics. Lenny Kravitz played out from my ipod as I tapped away on my keyboard, pouring out my thoughts and feelings for this book, I heard his lyrics sing out,

'There comes a time to be free of the heart, I'm gonna be ready, ready to start, on a love journey, got places to go, made up my mind, got to let you know . . . Heaven help the one who comes

in my life . . . Heaven help the fool who walks through my door, because I've decided right now I'm ready for love.'

They say that a woman reaches her sexual peak at forty and I was keen not to miss out on the experience. I felt I'd simply not had enough sex in my life and it was only fair that I got my designated quota! I wasn't ready for love again and had doubts whether I would ever seek that out in the future, but I was indeed ready for Luuuuve!

I've heard of a rather more crude term for it, but my sister Abby came up with a fitting name for what I was looking for, that being Date Buddies. My reasoning behind seeking multiple male acquaintances was that I'd be less likely to get emotionally attached, resulting in an inability to fall in love. My past experience of love had a historical outcome of unreliability, disappointment and lacked longevity. I simply felt very let down by the dream.

I had little idea of how and where I should start my search for these buddies. Although I am usually confident about my body and appearance, I confess to having some insecurities at that time. I was still recovering from recent breast surgery, having had my implants removed. I'd been left with a virtually flat chest and quite a bit of scarring. I hadn't been with another man other than Matt for eight years and by the nature of the ageing process, the body is naturally on the decline with regards to appearance as the years go by. To my credit, I remained attractive and maintained a good level of fitness. Although there were a few stretch marks and the skin looked less taut due to the decline of collagen, I was looking pretty good in comparison to many other women of my age.

As soon as my new found single status became public knowledge, I found a few of my married male friends changed their approach with me. With a cheeky glint in their eyes and flirtatious manner, I suspect they were probably sniffing around to see if they could discreetly assist me with my forty year old raging hormone disposition. Women also expressed an interest, with one dark horse sending me a text message after I'd innocently given her a lift home. The message from this Plain Jane character read,

Thanks for the lift! If you would like me to lick your pussy sometime, I would love you to sit on my face. If not, then hope all works out with your book. Thanks very much for the lift. Take care, xx

The sender later apologised if she had offended me with her forward text, claiming she had been very drunk at the time of sending it. I chuckled to myself. She was clearly not that drunk as she'd been able to tap out those words on the little keyboard of her phone and we all know that alcohol can serve as Truth Juice. Her text served as a flattering reminder that I was indeed attractive to both men and women. Needless to say, I chose not to take her up on the offer as my attentions were focused on the male species.

I started looking at male acquaintances in a different light, where previously I'd had my eyes closed to any obvious attractiveness. It was Martin that first caught my attention. I'd been using my local gym for several years and as routine set in, I became part of the furniture there, at the same time of day, three times a week. I'd see the same faces week after week and occasionally I'd get chatting to a few of the regular members.

I'd chat to Martin, who was in his early forties, over six feet tall, muscular, with a chiselled jaw line and thick dark brown hair. In a way, he reminded me a little of Matt. With a new mindset from my new found single status, I recognised that he was actually a really good looking guy. I quite fancied him, to the extent that my heart would race a little faster when he entered the gym at 5.15pm on the dot. I'd look forward to those rare moments when our exercise routines would result in us working out on equipment side by side, giving me the opportunity to spend a brief moment to chat to him. I'd discreetly spot him during his work out and go weak at the knees seeing the beads of sweat on the back of his neck.

I confided in my sister Tasha that I had the hots for Martin. I sought her advice on how I should go about asking him for a date, after all, I was out of practice in this game. I believed he was likely to be on the open market as I remembered him telling me that he'd split from a long term partner.

"Okay, we've given it a lot of thought and discussion," advised Tasha.

"We?" I questioned.

"Yes, I have discussed it in great detail with my male colleagues at work. Quite a few are your sort of age, so I decided that they would be best to talk to!" said Tasha in her frank, matter of fact tone.

"We have come up with several suggestions and we like your idea of putting a note on his car window, although we are a little concerned that you may appear to be the gym guys

stalker, by knowing what car he drives in the first place," she continued.

"Oh no, I don't think so. It's only a small car park and he has a distinctive enough car. I've seen him come and go in it enough times to rule out the stalker issue," I said in my defence. Although, I was now worried that I was displaying stalker like qualities, with my knowledge of his arrival times and the fact that I would secretly perv over his reflection in the mirror when he wasn't looking, or least I hope he wasn't!

"Your note to him should take the form of a lottery ticket with 'It's your lucky day' on the back of it. You then write your phone number on the ticket and invite him out for a drink," said Tasha, continuing with a couple of other suggestions, which I quickly rejected as they sounded too crude and forward, in contrast to the type of polite conversations I was accustomed to having with Martin.

The following day, I went to the shop to make my lottery ticket purchase. As I was not accustomed to filling out the form to select the numbers, I opted for the lucky dip and bought just the one ticket for the weekend draw. However, when I checked the back of the ticket, there was no phrase on it stating It's your lucky day, nor was there a space for me to write my invitation and telephone number on the back. I screwed the piece of paper up and as I got another two pound coin, I pushed the crumpled ticket into my purse. I bought two scratch cards, but now £3 down and I still didn't have anything saying It's your lucky day on it.

I contacted Tasha again,

"Where is it supposed to have printed on it, It's your lucky day?" I asked,

"No, it doesn't. You have to write that on the ticket yourself!" she giggled.

I decided to opt for the scratch card, as it seemed a little more heavy duty, I was not restricted with a time limit to get the note onto Martin's car and there was a space on the back to write what I needed to, by placing a sticker on the back of the 'how to play' obvious instruction details. In my neatest handwriting I wrote on the back of the scratch card, to include my number,

"IT'S YOUR LUCKY DAY—You win my phone number and may also win on this scratch card!! If you'd like to meet for a drink, then give me a call, Michelle x"

I kept the card in my car, complete with a waterproof covering and envelope, just in case it was to be fixed in place during a down pour, then commenced the waiting game.

In those days that followed, I waited in anticipation for Martin to be in the gym when I was there. I was intent on getting my timing right so that I could do my workout, then leave before him, with enough time to get that note on his car before he saw me fix it in place. I watched as the clock struck 5.10pm, guessing he'd be in at any moment, but then all that heart pounding was for nothing when by 5.30pm, he had not shown up and I'd have to wait yet another day.

It wasn't for about another week until I finally got my timing right and got that note on his car windscreen. About two hours later, my phone rang from an anonymous number. It was him! He was extremely lovely and polite, explaining that he was flattered by my note, thought the idea of the scratch card was really cool, but that he had recently met a really nice girl, so politely declined my offer. Bugger, bugger, bugger! was my initial thought. I hadn't predicted the scenario of him being with someone, having wrongly assumed he was single.

My disappointment quickly subsided as my friends suggested he'd probably have been far too boring for me, because he was the owner of a car more suited to a housewife and his reference to his want of a 'nice' girlfriend. The next time I saw him in the gym, I advised Martin that I had started an intensive course of counselling to deal with his rejection and that in time I would be able to get over him. We continued with our short friendly, between exercises conversations from then on and any embarrassment on my part was short lived.

My first sexual liaison in my new single life after Matt was undoubtedly with the wrong guy, but for many of the right reasons. I felt safe with Lawrence because he wasn't a random stranger. He knew all about my insecurities around my breast scars, was fully aware I hadn't been with a man since Matt and that I struggled to get my head around being intimate with someone new. I needed to feel confident, relaxed and sexy to get my kit off for any guy after this marriage break up. It's a big step to be with another guy after so many years being with just the one that you love. In the weeks before getting together with Lawrence, we were exchanging messages on Facebook. They began very innocently, enquiring how one another's day had gone. As time went on, Lawrence became more intense and I joked that I suspected he was grooming me. I had little interest in him at first, but that changed as he began to display a sensitive side that I warmed to. He would send me sweet thoughtful messages throughout the day, making me feel a little bit special and desirable. My sexual encounter with Lawrence ended up being a one off drunken, rather disappointing event. It was also an amazing momentous occasion, because this was sex after Matt and the start of new beginnings that I desperately wanted to progress with. I had been keen to get that first step out of the way so that I could move on from my feelings towards Matt.

Friends would frequently remind me that I was indeed a gorgeous person and suggest I must have a queue of handsome guys lining up for me. At first I thought I'd have no problems meeting new men because I had such a vivacious, flirtatious fun way about me (even if I say so myself!). I was indeed a confident person and enjoyed chatting up eligible guys. But that's the problem at forty, the men are usually married or with someone. At forty, I was no longer frequenting pubs and night clubs and even if I was to go to such venues, would be more likely to be surrounded by skinny lads in their twenties who I'd want to mother, rather than have sex with. So, I began my research into the dating websites and signed up to one that marketed itself around good looking women looking for financially secure, successful men.

I subscribed for a three month period and set about writing up my profile. I had to include a profile name, which I gave as Petra Kluske, but later changed it to the name Allure, a

name of a perfume I'm quite fond of. I tweaked my write up
several times, until it finally read;

*Life is so precious, everyday is a bonus and the best things are
for free!*

*First let me start by getting one thing clear. I am no gold digger.
I have no reason to be as I have a secure job and beautiful
home, complete with outdoor bar, perfect for my many dinner
parties! I am simply looking to find a guy (up to 45 years old)
who is financially stable. I did consider knocking a few years
off my profile age, but I'm proud of looking up together at 40.
I put in a lot of effort, going to the gym three times a week
(I pride myself on my abdominals) and I've recently started
rock climbing, which is a brilliant hobby. I have no children
and don't plan any. I'm loving life and happy about who I am.
Little Miss Independent . . . but keen to meet a guy who I can
meet up with a couple of times a month to share some exciting
adventure (basically, I have a full-time job and everyday
things to do that I'd struggle to have anymore free time!). The
luxury hotel or spa pampering doesn't thrill me—over-rated
and over-priced. I've nearly completed my first novel (it's all
about me!). I have no idea what's happening in the soaps as
the TV is rarely on. I prefer listening to music, any kind. I
love parties with a fancy dress theme—recent outfits include
Barbie, Trucker Girl (with Yorkie bar) Lady Ga-Ga, Wonder
Woman and Cat Woman! (The fantasy cop outfit is reserved
for private parties!). I find people have more fun when they
pretend to be someone else for one night only. I love travel
and have spent quite a bit of time in Australia and enjoy the
occasional City Break. I'm looking for a guy who is going to
enjoy my company, is adventurous and exciting, who looks
after themselves and sees the positive side to any situation.*

I had no problems selecting some photographs for my internet profile, as I'm never camera shy and love any opportunity to pose. I'm one of those people who take a good picture, but that's more likely to be because I ensure that loads of photographs are taken of me in a set pose, then delete any I deem substandard, leaving just a few remaining of me looking fabulous, which I save. I sussed out that it was a good idea to rotate photographs on a regular basis so that viewers revisited the profile, thinking it was a new person.

Once I'd paid my joining fee of around £15 a month, I had my advert in place. In a crude way it felt like I was putting myself up for sale, but could begin my own online shopping for a man. Within the first couple of days, the messages came pouring in from various characters. Many were much older guys who'd claim to have lots of money and appeared to think their apparent wealth may entice me into their company.

A guy with the profile name LordOscar sent me a message. Before opening it, I went to his profile to see a white haired man with a kindly, slightly chubby face, in a crisp white military uniform. He claimed to be fifty-three years old with an estate and yearly income of over a million pounds, university educated, six feet tall and looking for his soul mate. He made reference to life being precious, which had also been a line in my own write-up. He made mention of owning several homes around the world, describing himself as a world traveller and currently on his boat in a hot sunny location.

His message to me read,

Hi,

I enjoyed reading your profile. You sound like a lot of fun. Please check out my profile and if you are interested do write back. With warmest regards from sunny Spain, Oscar x

I wrote back to Oscar, thanking him for his message, explaining that I didn't feel we were a match, but wished him the very best in his search for his ideal girl.

Although I wasn't expecting it, Oscar replied back to my message of rejection.

Thankyou very much for taking the time, trouble and effort to write your message. You are very sweet. If you ever have the urge to date a Grandpa like me, I would certainly give you a run for your money anytime, like you have no idea . . .

Anyway, I wish you luck in your quest.

A charismatic lady with a good heart.

Besos from Spain, Oscar, x

I never communicated with Oscar after his last message, but his ears must have been burning as he became the topic of entertaining conversation between my friends and I one evening. As the wine was flowing, one of my friends spoke of being in desperate need of a holiday, then another said she'd like to go too. Before we knew it, we'd come up with a great plan, that we'd contact Oscar and asked if he'd like to have four gorgeous girls on his boat for a week. He would reap the benefits of being able to perv over us as we sunbathe topless.

We considered that he may also like to pay for our flights, but then felt such a gesture was worth more than watching a bit of topless sunbathing. We considered that one of us may need to offer Oscar a little more to repay his generosity. If so, it would need to be in the dark because he looked old, certainly older than fifty-three. It was decided that I'd have to take responsibility if there was any hanky panky to be done, as he had expressed the interest in me. After much debate, we concluded that it wasn't actually worth it and we didn't really want to go on his boat anyway!

I started to get a lot of messages and began corresponding with quite a few guys. However, I was all too aware that on the internet we can be whoever we want to be, so when I was interested in a guy I'd do some research. I kept a book, dedicating a page to each guy that had some potential. I'd recording relevant information about them, so that I didn't get them mixed up. Google is such a fantastic tool and I would suggest that any woman do all she can to find out about her date before they meet. Women need to take their personal safety into account when they meet a date. Searching for information about them allows for a better risk assessment.

Indeed, there are a few of those who are likely to be the fraudsters and scammers. Such guys will display a gorgeous looking profile picture, claim to be loaded and sound like a dream. As the messages begin, they will quickly declare their undying love for the female. Then, they will say they are away on business in some remote country, have become stranded and ask for help. That's when the vulnerable female sends vast sums of money via MoneyGram or Western Union, never to see the return of their wealth again.

There is something called LinkedIn, a professional networking site used by many employed in fields such as finance, IT, marketing and the self-employed. I joined this site claiming at that time to be an author, which enabled me to interrogate information stored about some of the potential dates. I noticed that some guys used the same profile picture that they had displayed on LinkedIn. This helped me to identify that I'd located the right subject. If I got an e-mail address for the guy, I was able to do a check on Google, Facebook and LinkedIn. A mobile number was good to search, anything that pinned a person down with some individual information.

I was able to find out a surname of one potential date by putting his profile nickname into Google. I found this was a name he also used on Twitter. I then searched LinkedIn and found out where he worked and what position he held within the corporate company. I felt safer with the knowledge that I knew as much as possible before meeting a potential date. That way, I'd also know if he was spinning me a yarn about his himself. If a woman feels safe and comfortable, then the date is more likely to be a success.

I got a few messages from married men. One was a thirty-two year old, with a profile name NiceGuy and with a rather unattractive picture attached. His profile read,

Just a guy who needs some excitement as I'm bored of the same old work and no play. It's time for me to play! I spend my time between London and America. I want to be honest, so confess that I am not single. I'd like to meet someone for some no strings attached fun!

His message to me read,

Hi there, you are stunning!! So let's cut to the chase lol . . . what's it going to take to get my hands on those curves of yours? . . .

I was tempted to write back the following,

How dare you even think you are in my league! If you'd looked at my profile pictures properly, you'd see that I am not that curvy and a creep like you isn't going to get their hands on me at any price. I'm not for sale!

Instead, I pressed the delete button to his message and went on to the next.

It was the profile of Aries121, that caught my eye. He was a tall, handsome looking forty-two year old IT Manager, with thick dark hair, who displayed a smart corporate photograph of himself in a pin striped suit. I started messaging him and established that Simon lived near Tasha. I could incorporate a trip to see my sister and go for a date with Simon, feeling safe with the knowledge that Tasha would be nearby if he turned out to be weird.

After several e-mails and texts, Simon and I arranged our date for a Tuesday, when I had the week off work. I was so excited about the date and wanted to make sure I looked absolutely gorgeous. On the Monday, I got my nails manicured, had a full body professional tan applied and left it on overnight to fully develop.

I struggled to sleep on the Monday night because I was so looking forward to meeting Simon, my first internet date.

When my alarm sounded at 7am, I jumped out of bed and threw on my gym kit, feeling a fitness session that morning would ensure I looked toned and fabulous for that evening. As I prepared my breakfast, I became aware of a pain deep down in my stomach. At first I shrugged it off and thought I'd feel okay once I had breakfast. However, the pain was preventing me from pouring the milk in my tea, let alone chopping up my banana for my porridge. I decided to open the front door, just on case I passed out. I didn't want my door kicked in! I picked up my mobile phone and carried it as I walked around the house, contorting myself into various positions in an attempt the ease the pain. The last time I'd felt anything similar to this, I'd ended up in hospital having my fallopian tubes operated on.

I'd known things weren't quite right for a couple of weeks, since discovering that I had a movable lump in my stomach. Although I'd been back and forth to the surgery, doctors had been unable to diagnose what was wrong. I'd been calling the lump my unborn alien baby, but I'd noticed in my doctors notes that it had been written up as questioning STOMACH DISEASE. I found this disturbing as I interpreted the word disease, perhaps naively, with the thought that the condition wasn't going to go away.

I went upstairs, climbed onto my bed, positioning myself on my hands and knees and had my mobile phone beside me. I started to feel scared. What if I was about to die from my stomach disease? I had a date to go on and I was so looking forward to it. I wasn't ready to die just yet!

I have spent years dealing with everyone else's emergencies, yet here I was with a drama of my own. I kept looking at my phone and knew the three buttons I needed to press. But, I knew that as soon as I did, my hopes for my date with Simon that evening were over. I didn't want to miss out on the date! I didn't want to pass out, then die because I hadn't called for help in time!

I knew I had no choice but to do it, and so I did. As I dialled 999 and asked for the ambulance, I was consumed with disappointment and pain. I feared I could pass out from the pain at any moment, so got busy, sending text messages to Simon to cancel the date and to Matt to let him know of my emergency. Matt and I were no longer together, but I did still consider him to be my best friend.

I remember little about my arrival in hospital, because I was all consumed with pain and had been pumped with morphine in the ambulance. Matt must have dropped everything to get to me for my arrival in hospital. It was a comfort to have him there, because he cared.

The pain remained relentless and was so extreme that I would rather have died than be forever with that suffering. As I waited for a scan, I felt so distressed. The intense ache wouldn't let up and the cannula was pulling on my skin. Doctors suspected I had a hernia and one took to pressing down on the lump protruding from my stomach. This caused me such immense pain that I couldn't stop myself snapping with a few chosen F words, to voice my displeasure.

The scan revealed I had a cyst, rather than a hernia. In fact, the pressing on the lump could have burst the cyst! I became suspicious of the doctors and whether I was in safe hands or not. That said, I trusted the nursing staff. Their patience and kindness was unfaltering.

I was told the cyst was in my stomach and was twelve centimetres round, so about the size of a Cantaloupe melon! It was referred to as a rare mesenteric cyst. Consideration was given to operating on me there and then, as the starvation process had commenced with my nil by mouth status. Although I was feeling terrible, as the hours went on, I was looking better and better, as if I'd just been away on a two week holiday in the Caribbean. My fake tan should have been washed off hours ago, yet was continuing to develop and glow, leaving me looking deceptively healthy and fabulous!

Finally, the decision was made for me to be discharged from hospital. I was to return within a few weeks to have this alien baby chopped out for good. It's a shame I wasn't operated on there and then, because the ten day wait that followed, consumed me with thoughts and fears of what was going to take place. I'd been told the cyst was in my stomach, so I contemplated that complications may result in me needing to have a colostomy bag. I Googled colostomy bags and considered the impact this would have on me getting it together with a guy in the future.

I knew either way that I'd be left with a huge scar across my stomach, just above the waist line. I was gutted to hear this as I had quite enough scars to be getting on with. This one was to be positioned in the place I prided myself the most, my muscular abdominal area.

I considered how I'd hide up such unattractiveness. I felt I'd need to turn to using sexy underwear to conceal my scars.

As I thought more about this, I decided it wasn't all bad. I doubted a guy was going to complain if I was insistent on wearing black lace and stockings! I'm not sure that they'd go much on the colostomy bag though, even with a black lace covering.

There's no denying that I was scared about having the operation and fearful that the cyst may be something sinister, life changing and perhaps life ending. I didn't let on to my friends that I was petrified. I concealed my fear by joking about the impending birth of my alien baby by C-section.

I was somewhat relieved when I came out of the operating theatre to be told the cyst hadn't been in my intestine after all. Surgeons had discovered that the highly mobile mass had been attached to my ovary. I'd been plagued by the bloody cysts during my IVF days and this big bugger had come along with a vengeance. It had not been removed in isolation because most of my ovary had to be taken away with it. I had no intention of ever pursuing IVF again, so didn't actually need my ovaries to procreate, but I was only too aware of the role of the ovaries.

A new set of fears faced me with the interference of hormone balance. Was I now to be gifted with beard growth? I'd been having my periods far too frequently and knew my hormones were already out of sync. The doctor reassured me that the other ovary would compensate and beard growth wouldn't be expected. But, I wasn't sure, because by now, I didn't really trust what the doctors were telling me. They'd got it wrong a few too many times already for my liking. Not forgetting that weeks prior to my operation, I'd been told that scan results had shown my ovaries were "fine" and the huge attachment to one of them hadn't even been spotted.

As for the scar that the seven inch incision had left behind, I decided that I was going to love it. It was very visible, sitting horizontally just below my belly button, but I thought it looked a bit rock'n'roll. It left its mark as a reminder that you never know what's around the corner and that life is indeed precious and health the greatest wealth.

Recovery from such an operation was forecast to be slow and I was disappointed that I was actually in more pain after surgery, than I had been before the cyst removal. The repair process was slow and I was confined to home for much of the time during my recovery. I had to wait for weeks for the biopsy results and I couldn't rule out that the cyst removal may not be the end of my health concerns.

I was keen for a distraction and my computer offered just that. The internet served as a great source of amusement as I convalesced in my comfy chair, with my lap top on, scanning the dating site for only the gorgeous guys. I knew in the back of my mind that my health was delaying any actual dates, but it was indeed fun searching to see what was available.

CHAPTER NINETEEN

INCREDIBLE, YOU ARE AMAZING

"*Babe, you look gorgeous, everyone's looking at you, you know, because you are so stunning!*" said Ryan, full of gushing compliments as usual.

'© *By Photographer, Sophie Rossi*'

"*I've told my lesbian friends all about you and that I'm out with you today. They want me to send them a photo. They hope you might fancy one of them. I've told them you're bi!"* continued Ryan.

"That was a long time ago. I'm not that fussed about the chick thing now. I think I might be over it, after all, I did turn down Plain Jane," I said.

"Oh Hun, that was so funny! I can't believe she sent you that text! She was really into you, you know. How did you reply to that?" asked Ryan.

"Well, I sent a text to thank her for her kind offer and asked if I could bank it," I said, trying to hold together a serious face.

"Really Babe? She's got nice boobs though . . ." said Ryan.

"No, of course I didn't say I wanted to bank it!" I scorned. *"She is definitely not my type, with or without the nice set of top bollocks! Besides, I have a couple of possible dates lined up with some hot guys,"* I said.

I expect Ryan and I were keeping everyone entertained by our conversation as we queued up for our all you can eat carvery. We'd liken the venue to a bit of a soup kitchen, but we loved it. Our lunch date was set in a pretty pub beside a lake, where we could get a huge dinner and a drink for less than a fiver. We found our table and tucked into our feast, whilst gossiping and giggling about the most stupid of things, as usual.

I told Ryan that I thought dating should be likened to house hunting. I think many of us make so little effort to find our soul mate. We meet someone at work, or through friends.

Perhaps we meet during a drunken night out or our eyes meet in Tescos and we call it fate. We go on a few dates and get on well. Before we know it, we're officially an item and the wedding cake is on order.

However, if we were to go in search for our dream home, any estate agent would suggest that we get loads of property details, go for lots of viewings, arrange second viewings, perhaps even a third, before progressing with a survey. Only once we are completely happy, we then go ahead with the purchase. Sometimes, at that crucial point when we're about to exchange contracts, we suddenly see a better property has arrived on the market and pull out from the deal. Perhaps the seller of our dream home decides they are no longer wanting to move out.

I considered taking this analogy into the realms of dating. This would of course would mean I'd have to be a serial dater, in search of nothing less than my Penthouse Show Home. I wasn't really sure I wanted to move into a Penthouse just yet, but I was keen to have some fun seeing what was on the market.

I told Ryan that I'd joined an internet dating site and that I'd definitely had my monies worth in entertainment value in the few weeks I'd been doing it. I'd only been on one coffee date so far and I'd been flirting with a few of the guys via text. The signal wasn't great in the pub, but we sat patiently, waiting for my phone to load up the website, so I could show Ryan my shopping basket of men.

Roger was forty-four years old, so almost out of my set criteria. He apparently had a good income and sounded wonderful in his profile write up. He was divorced and had two teenaged daughters who he had contact with every other week, so I felt he wouldn't be too demanding of my time, should he become one of my date buddies. He would no doubt be taking me to affluent places to meet intellectual people that I would never get to encounter in my world. He sounded quite a catch. However, there was just one problem. His photo. He didn't look hot at all. Ryan and I examined the image further, zooming in to seek out the finest of details. As we did, the picture became distorted and blurred.

"Babe, I need to draw your attention to this . . . It looks like a possible comb over flapping in the wind," said Ryan, zooming into Roger's head.

We looked closer and I felt a little cheated that his profile described his hair as blonde, yet we could definitely detect ginger tones. His skin looked rather old, leathered and dimpled, but this could make him look rugged. Perhaps he may have a sexy tone to his voice and the most charismatic way about him. I looked again at the photo,

"Mmmmm, I'm not sure I could get jiggy with Mr ginger haired protruding chin, with or without him buying me lovely gifts and taking me to fabulous places. No, I can't do it. Nop, just can't. It makes me feel a bit sick actually. Let's move onto the next!" I said.

We continued to go through the different faces, zooming in and being the harshest of critics. I felt that Pete might be my favourite, but Ryan wasn't too sure about his dress sense, spotting that Pete was wearing a T-shirt under a suit jacket in one of his photographs. I actually liked that look and regardless of Ryan's views, I thought Pete looked cute. We flicked onto Sean and once again scrutinised the photo and our flurry of messages to one another, analysing his responses to assess what we thought he was going to be like in person.

"Well, I really like that one. I think he is going to be husband number four. I can feel it in my arthritic bones," I giggled.

"Hun, you just love that wedding cake don't you! You love those weddings and being the centre of attention for the day!" sniggered Ryan.

"At least I can say I've done the top three. I've done the church, registry office and beach weddings, but the irony is that no one's ever actually got down on one knee and proposed to me! We've just sort of decided to get married," I said in a slightly disappointed tone.

"Oh Hun, there's still time yet for your dream marriage proposal! You should do a Vegas drive through next time, or maybe one of those bungee jump weddings," suggested Ryan.

"The problem is that I've only got to kiss a guy, then that's it, I fall in love and have got to marry him. I've only ever kissed three guys in my life and they've all ended up being my husband! . . . Shall we get an ice-cream?" I said.

It was a bank breaking £1.99 for the soft serve ice-cream, from a 'help yourself to as much as you like' machine. Ryan and I were quite happy to sit for hours refilling our bowls at intervals. We'd pour on loads of chocolate sauce over our swirly delight then stuff our faces with the frozen dessert until we felt a bit sick from over-indulgence. It didn't get much better than that, not for all the money in the world!

I scambled around for a two pound coin and decided my purse was in need of a clear out for all those annoying receipts that filled it so unnecessarily. It was only then that I came across a crumpled lottery ticket.

"I forgot all about this!" I said, unfolding the ticket and smoothing it out flat on the table, as it soaked up a bit of melted ice and a splatter of gravy.

Ryan began tapping on his phone to search the web for historical lottery results. But, the signal was poor and I was tempted to give up and throw it away. Besides, what's the chances of a win? Especially for someone as Lucky, Lucky, Lucky as me!

"If I win, then we'll split the money my lovely," I announced.

"No, you couldn't do that. Just let me come on holiday with you on your yacht or something! Champagne for everyone! Whoooop Whoooop!!" said Ryan.

"I wouldn't need all the money, because I'd be dating some rich guy who would be buying me all the diamonds and pearls I'd need." I joked.

I contemplated what I'd actually do if I was to come into lots of money. I'd pack up work, not because I disliked what I did, but because it took up so much of my life. I'd rather be doing something else like travelling to see the World. I'd want to keep my home because I liked it there. I might have a few other homes in addition, but I wouldn't be fussed. I'd get my Botox and lip fillers done more often and spend lots of time in the beauty salon, but I wasn't really sure.

"You know, Ryan, when I wake in the morning, Darius sings to me. He tells me that I'm incredible and amazing. Then when I go to bed at night, I say a little prayer. I don't really know who I'm saying it to because I don't know if there is a God or not, but I say it anyway. I say 'Thank you God, my life is brilliant'. I really do you know!" I said.

"It's linked into the National Lottery website now Babe," said Ryan.

"There's a saying that goes something like . . ., health is the greatest gift, contentment the greatest wealth and faithfulness the best relationship. All the money in the world can't buy that. So, what are the numbers then?" I asked.

"Seven"
"Yep, got that"
"Twenty three"
"Yes, that's here"
"Twenty nine"
"How funny! I've got that as well!!!!!"
"Forty" . . .

www.ingramcontent.com/pod-product-compliance
Lightning Source LLC
Chambersburg PA
CBHW061340280526
45784CB00001B/82